Angelettes
&
Cosmic Sex

FURTHER CONSPIRACIES?!

If you would like to read further on the New Age Conspiracy to elevate Human Consciousness on this Planet and elsewhere—don't simply ask your book dealer to order the following titles—Demand that S/He do so! They are:

THE FUTURE HISTORY SERIES
By Timothy Leary, Ph.D.
Info-Psychology
Neuropolitique
The Intelligence Agents
What Does WoMan Want?
Millennium Madness
The Game Of Life

THE ROBERT ANTON WILSON SERIES
The Cosmic Trigger
Sex and Drugs
Wilhelm Reich In Hell
Prometheus Rising
Coincidance—A New Anthology
Ishtar Rising: Book of the Breast

THE FUTURE IS *NOW* SERIES

Undoing Yourself With Energized Meditation and Other Devices • By Christopher S. Hyatt, Ph.D., Introduced by Israel Regardie, Extensive Foreword by Robert Anton Wilson.
A Modern Shaman's Guide to a Pregnant Universe • by C.S. Hyatt, Ph.D. & Antero Alli
Breaking The GodSpell: Genetic Evolution • by Neil Freer, Introduced by Zecharia Sitchin.
The Sapiens System—The Illuminati Conspiracy: Their Objectives, Methods & Who They Are! • By Donald Holmes, M.D., Extensive Introduction by Robert Anton Wilson.
Angel Tech: A Modern Shaman's Guide to Reality Selection • by Antero Alli, Preface by Robert Anton Wilson.
All Rites Reversed?!: Ritual Technology for Self-Initiation • by Antero Alli
Zen Without Zen Masters • by Camden Benares.
Monsters and Magical Sticks: There Is No Such Thing As Hypnosis? • By Steven Heller, Ph.D., Introduced by Robert Anton Wilson
The Cybernetic Conspiracy (Mind Over Matter) • by Constantin Negoita, Ph.D.
An Extraterrestrial Conspiracy • by Marian Greenberg
The Shaman Warrior • by Gini Graham Scott, Ph.D.
A Search for Meaning: Towards a Psychology of Fulfillment • by Alan Garner
Power and Empowerment • by Lynn Atkinson, Ph.D.
The Dream Illuminati Vimana Conspiracy • by Wayne Saalman, Introduced by Robert Anton Wilson
Mega-Babies: Baby Boomers are Booming • by Timothy Leary, Ph.D., C.S. Hyatt, Ph.D., & Linda Miller, R.N., B.S.N.
Angelettes and Cosmic Sex • by Pusser
RX Shiksa • by J.R. Ephraim
Blue Star • by Bonnie Hadley

Don't forget **THE JUNGIAN PSYCHOLOGY SERIES**
THE GOLDEN DAWN SERIES • THE ALEISTER CROWLEY SERIES

For a free catalog of all Falcon titles contact:

FALCON PRESS
1209 South Casino Center, Suite 147 • Las Vegas, NV 89104
702-385-5749

Angelettes & Cosmic Sex

by
Pusser

FALCON PRESS
LAS VEGAS, NEVADA

Copyright ©1989 Pusser

All rights reserved. No part of this book, in part or in whole, may be reproduced, transmitted or utilized, in any form or by any means, electronic or mechanical, including photocopying, recording, or by any information storage and retrieval system, without permission in writing from the publisher, except for brief quotations in critical articles and reviews.

International Standard Book Number: 0-941404-86-2
Library of Congress Catalog Card Number: 88-081436

First edition – 1989
Published by Falcon Press

Book Design, Typography and Production by
RapidScribe Communications
A division of
Studio 31/Royal Type
27 West 20th Street • Room 1005
New York, NY 10011

Cover Painting by Sallie Ann Glassman
Cover Design by Studio 31

FALCON PRESS
1209 South Casino Center, Suite 147
Las Vegas, Nevada 89104
1-702-385-5749

Manufactured in the United States of America

Contents

Introduction 1
Chapter I 3
Chapter II 9
Chapter III 17
Chapter IV 23
Chapter V 31
Chapter VI 39
Chapter VII 47
Chapter VIII 53
Chapter IX 63
Chapter X 73
Chapter XI 81
Chapter XII 89
Chapter XIII 95
Chapter XIV 101

Introduction

There is a new age of Spiritualism opening, which is available to us all. You must open your heart and mind, and know that we are evolving, but are not yet Gods. Rather, we are the precious seeds of Star Children of the one God.

"As above, so below." As the acorn can become the oak with nurturing and light, so we can open to the Kingdoms of Light; but we must grow, change, and adapt, as evolution directs.

To say we are all that is to be, is to limit the paths that are open to us. The virtues of your own developed Ego creates paths, but the distortion of pride can cut the crossroads, and slow the evolutionary process. Knowing that God is omniscient and omnipotent, we also realize that he changes his forms of expression through those individualized expressions we term humankind. As such, we have our own dazzling destinies to devise.

We must plan and plod our paths, for then we fulfill our evolution by becoming pioneers of the worlds and planes of consciousness which each new imagination describes. Man was given an individualized consciousness through which he can adapt and mold this planet; nevertheless, he is responsible for the caring of this orb called Earth, and not its anointed king.

We must take in the perspectives of the heavens through our physical eyes, and view the whole in a new light; seeing and appreciating our different myriad concepts of existence and permutations of imaginations, which encompass all evolved creation.

God is there for all who seek Him, in all the manifestations attributed to Him; and in those, all our combined realities remain to be yet discovered. Enlightened men know that all of our conscious thoughts combined on Earth constitute but a fraction of His Being.

As the acorn evolving to the oak is but a fraction of the forest chain of life, and the whole chain is dependent on each of its parts; so all must be connected together for any to bud, grow, die, and rebud, in the cycles of evolution and growth.

Whatever fraction, you are an important integrated part of the whole, and as responsible to those above, as to those behind you. An Enlightened Age must include sharing Light and knowledge with those in darkness, so that through sharing, a balancing of understanding occurs in all. This is the only way for the Divine Seed to bud, thereby giving deeper spiritual awareness. Night and day are both needed in balanced proportions to stimulate and maintain growth: either one without the other, or present in conflicting intervals, would prevent the bud of cyclic existence from blooming.

We are the creative caretakers of Earth and must refine our realities and rechannel relationships with all life: nature, animals, and those in an unbalanced state, so that our single and combined paths can achieve the equilibrium and maximum destiny potential for each. Do not be lost at the crossroads by centering all realities on your own reflections. When man learned that Earth was not the center of this solar system, he should have assimilated "as above, so below", and consequently recognized the corresponding position he fallaciously assigned in his own Ego in relation to the Creator. We must grow together with our united spirits defined by our resplendent separate identities, blended into evolved consciousness and spiritual openness. Then, and only then, will our chain of life on Earth exist in harmony and balance; and the New Age be realized by all.

I

The street was dark and grimy, and the wind shrieked past the tall buildings reflecting many images of active decay.

With hands clenched in their pockets, two women huddled in their jackets, and directed their attention toward the ground strewn with garbage and dog excrement. It was safer to look down than acknowledge the vacant stares of the people in the neighborhood.

"Laurel, why do you insist we go to this new place?" the taller and plainer of the pair asked. "You always come up with the kinkiest experiences: those that satisfy you, and alarm me."

"Evelyn, you might dress as the plainest, most unfeminine woman around, but your curiosity is your passion: it is always aroused. You are more alarmed when I don't show you the many unusual aspects of life," the buxom redhead answered.

"I suppose femininity to you is related to your makeup, perfumes, and most importantly, your breasts. To me, it is the receptive force instead of the aggressive one. I am alarmed by the depravity of people: the dark side; but it is my pleasure, my femininity, to record in my mind all facets of human nature and experiences. My sanity lies in watching life," Evelyn admitted.

"Watching is your pleasure, yes, but when do you let go? It's been years Evelyn since you've let go to participate; but I feel this place holds a special thrill for both of us. This is different: free love yes, but the male members are aliens.

There's even an alien Prince," Laurel gushed in her excitement.

"An alien stud! How fortunate for you, Laurel. An experience very few others could duplicate. You're fucking E.T.," Evelyn laughed.

"Evelyn, don't be crude! He's magnificent, the Prince; and the others are beautiful also. They are superior beings from other worlds, and they are here to impregnate those deserving to be Mothers of the new race," Laurel replied.

But Evelyn continued to laugh. "Mothers of a new race. This is a new experience for you. This time you'll leave with more than organ secretions, your normal reward for pleasures. The Mother of a new race who just about fucked herself through the old one."

Laurel laughed also. "Oh Evelyn, I love your sense of humor. I have often thought of motherhood."

"Sure you have Laurel, when you've gone to the abortion clinic, and when you ran out of pills. So now you're going to mother an alien child. What are you thinking, that this will improve your image?"

Evelyn, you're a great judge of emotions and minds. That's why I always want you around watching. You see things I and others miss; besides, you're the best lawyer I know. Can't you sense my sincerity?"

"I sense your sincerity Laurel; it's the aliens' motives I'm questioning."

"Oh Evelyn you didn't question if they're aliens or not," Laurel replied happily.

"I sense you believe they are aliens, Laurel. What they are to my mind remains to be seen."

They approached the chipped cement steps leading to a tenement that reeked of urine, and the condensing sweat of fear. As they entered the dimly lit building and walked down the dank hallway, the odors of incense and the drone of chanting assailed their senses.

Evelyn felt as if she were entering an alien environment. There was a pressure in the air that set off alarm signals throughout her consciousness. Evelyn thought, what is alien? Alien to a planet, or alien to one's experiences: the narrower the view, the more things appear alien; the more knowledge, the more relation between all things. Fear is the alien emotion, unexplained and undefined. All her senses were heightened.

The apartment was opened by a young black male, dressed as an African chief, with feathers and bones entwined in his massive hair. He recognized Laurel, and bade them entry with a smile, pointing his finger forward.

Laurel and Evelyn entered a large room crammed with people and animals, and alive with noises and smells. Evelyn looked at the male aliens curiously. All of them were glorious physical specimens from all of the races: white, black, red, yellow, and brown. They were mixed in pairs and groups, and their sexual positions were incredible.

"Evelyn, why are you looking so intense? Since when did collective copulation so affect you?"

"Thanks for bringing me back to myself. It isn't the sex or disorder. There is something tangible here: something I find disturbing," Evelyn admitted.

"Look over there, Evelyn. That's what I call disturbing. There's the Prince. Isn't he out of this world?"

Evelyn noticed the object of her friend's attention. He was enormous: about 6'6", with white skin, and covered completely with a mass of thick, black hair. His penis was equally large in proportion. He was naked, aloof, and erect as a stud horse. A group of women gathered in front of him.

Laurel said, "Oh! we just made it. The Prince is about to pick his partner for the evening. He chooses only one woman a session: everyone else interchanges and goes to different groupings. The Prince fucks one girl silly, giving her much of his seed. His breeding is different than the others. How I wish he would pick me!"

The guru, an old naked Indian seated on the dais at the back of the room, spoke. "Since the dawn of planet Earth's time, more evolved beings have come to Earth to take their pleasure and plant the seeds of children of higher consciousness to improve Humankind. We have come from other worlds to give you our strength and knowledge, to be passed onto our children. These children will be superior to simple Earthlings. They will develop great powers, and eventually rule this planet. This perfection of our race can mingle with yours, as we offer you the seed of the future."

"Laurel, you can't believe that," Evelyn pleaded.

"Why can't I believe? Look at them; each a perfect example of health and vitality. And the Prince, can't you feel the power and energies emanating from him? You are an expert on human nature. Don't you feel the extraordinary powers he produces? Isn't he above human nature as we know it?" Laurel beamed as she looked at the Prince.

"You're right about the sense of power," Evelyn answered. "I do feel an intense building of power: energy under pressure, but alien races improving Earthlings? Look at the women here who are the chosen recipients. You and the rest are not exactly the type I would expect a superior being would choose to mother his children. The females here are all pleasure seekers: they show the physical strains of abused flesh, and the emotional scars of hedonism. Think about it honestly, Laurel. Why would an alien choose you?"

Chosen is the key word tonight. My lust for the Prince is enormous. He's ready to pick, and I want his prick. You're on your own now," Laurel replied as she walked to the group surrounding the Prince.

"Now, the ultimate spectator experience. Women having sex with aliens and nurturing a new race. My God! they can't really believe it!" Evelyn wondered aloud.

"People believe exactly what they want to. To some reality extends only to the limits of their pleasures; and through pleasure alone, they vainly seek to expand their reality," responded an old man with a long white beard and sparkling blue eyes. He wore a long white robe; he and Evelyn were the only two not naked. "Who are you, an alien philosopher?" quipped Evelyn.

"Aliens are beings that cannot align with the whole. To be in tune with unity is to be a part of everything, whether it involves your original birth planet or not. To be fragmented and only self-directed is to be alien everywhere," the man answered.

"I sense you are not an alien. Are the others?" she asked.

"Yes, they are aliens. Though it is not the point of origin of energy that alienates it; it can go the reaches of the universe and return to the center with more facets in harmony. But an energy or entity that cannot find the harmony of its pattern within the Harmony of the universe is alien. These beings here expend great spurts of energy, but they are not in harmony with the pattern, for self-adulation loses sight of the pattern. So the energy bursts strongly, but illuminates little, and returns to darkness, not Light. Only in Light is the sustenance and continuity of the future and Evolution. In the Light you are never an alien, though you travel the far distant galaxies. So, they do not lie about that; they are aliens everywhere. Not because they come from other worlds, as we both do, but because they are not creating a world of harmony, but one of pleasure and power for their own egos. They are aliens in all worlds; they are aliens of evolution. Come, I have something to show you."

They entered the next room, illuminated by a few flickering candles which muted the garish walls. The only thing clearly discernible was a large mirror which covered one wall. The old man sat in front of it and gestured to Evelyn to do the same. He looked at her and stated, "Can you look into the Mirror of

Life: the Mirror of the Past? Look into the mirror and learn."

Evelyn looked into the mirror and heard him repeat the phrases. She had a sensation of dizziness, and envisioned a white mist penetrating her consciousness. She could feel her mind expanding, but had no control over the sense of speed or the direction.

II

This was a garden of delights, lush and tropical with an over abundance of sensual stimuli: the fragrance of flowers, chirping of birds, clamor of insects in crescendo, springy grasses, the sun radiating warmth and heat, and a cool crisp river flowing through the lush green surroundings.

A mother and child sat by the water, and an older man with a white beard and sparkling eyes sat on the knoll above watching them. All three had translucent skin which radiated all the colors of the prism. The mother had long, flowing red hair, and was naked beneath two layers of veils: one silver, one gold. The child wore a green veil, and both had medallions consisting of two crossed crescent moons with a six pointed star on the apex, and a five pointed star on the nadir, hanging over their hearts.

"I love you, my daughter Mariella. Many changes of evolution will come before we meet again. I tell you today of your destiny and of your heritage. They are your future.

"I come from worlds far away from Earth. We are an older race of beings who have long since passed the stages of physical evolvement. We are the caretakers of Evolutions: we oversee galaxies and life forms enumerous. We are the Light and the brightness.

"When the Great Father infused into matter and gave a human child to the planet Earth, many of us were inspired to do the same. The limitation and concentration of great energy forces can create life and further the cycle of The Great Evolution, of which we are all a part.

"Your father is Michael, the Archangel of Light. He and I took physical forms, and mated in the Garden of Birth on Earth.

"Your father and I were riding the universe on a crest of love and blazing comets. While we were travelling out of these Earth forms, Luciel, Michael's brother, implanted another seed in my womb.

"This was not mating, for it had no conscious alignment with the energy of the cosmos. Rather, it was Luciel's way of forcing his participation in the event. He has always been self-centered, instead of whole-centered.

"When I returned to Earth body, I had two seeds: you and your brother. I felt the unbalance Luciel created, but I aligned your brother to the whole, and then you and he were aligned together. This so angered Luciel that upon your births, he stole your brother Lucien from me. He keeps him to himself, and only during Earth Reincarnations, which Luciel cannot break, can the energy patterns of you and your brother realign this unbalance. As such, it is your destiny to redress this disharmony.

"You must find your brother, each of you in your Earth incarnations, and mate with him to give balance to Earth and its evolution. You will reincarnate as individual souls of different cultures, for when the individual parts of the whole reunite in mating, they reaffirm the Light of the whole. You are of the root Races of Earth, and as you grow so does your planet and all therein. When you and Lucien mate, you will realign the spirit of yourselves, of me, of your Fathers, and most importantly, of Earth: the planet of your destiny.

"Evolution is many changes and many growths. When the old growth achieves its potential it becomes inert, and must then be subjected to great change and new stimuli to help it progress to new realms. This is the Law of Evolution: the Law of Planets, and correspondingly, the Law of Individual Life Cycles.

"The Planet Earth will have Great Changes to stimulate the growth of the root races: seven cycles of Earth, seven cycles of Great Change, seven root Races of Man.

"All in life have a purpose; and all purpose stems from the center. Luciel is an Archangel who lost sight of the whole while working on the dissection of its parts, and in concentration on the parts, lost understanding of its function as a whole. Only he would allow perfect development of individual parts, but perfection is a static energy: it has no room for growth and evolution. Perfection negates the concept of Evolution.

"The individual parts must be developed, but then the individual must be sacrificed for the whole. Wholeness is to take what you have developed by yourself, and then to use it by giving it to all life around you: your brother, your planet, all humans, all life. The energy of life evolution goes forward as all of its parts progress together: some at fast rates of speed, others slow; but all pulsing toward the same center.

"Luciel believes in 'adapt or die'. He encourages races and individuals to develop for their own egos: that is his precept of perfection. He believes this planet and the races of Earth are inferior, and he helps create great unbalanced surges of energy by fragmenting its parts and feeding illusions.

"These great surges of unbalance energies are an integral part of Earth's destiny, and the reason for Luciel's assignment. This flux of force produces the stimulus and change that is the death of the old, in order to give rebirth to the new.

"Luciel tries to prevent the rebirth, though he gladly leads Earth to the death which precedes it. When you find your brother and mate with him, you realign the energy flux and assist the rebirth, which is your destiny. You and he will be born to Earth at the same moment, yet miles apart. You will always incarnate before the Cycle of Great Change, so you can find your brother and together mate, to reroute and redefine the energy patterns that flux into earthquakes, floods, tornadoes and all of nature's fury of imbalance. All excess energies must be combined, or die to be reborn in the new cycle.

"Luciel will try to prevent your mating with your brother, for this realigns your brother with the whole, and Luciel would have him only for himself. Between earth incarnations, Luciel feeds Lucien with self-pride and fragmentation. You are his way back to the center. You are the knowledge to temper his experiences.

"To protect you from Luciel on Earth, you will be unaware of your power and heritage until you are an adult, and ready to find your brother on Earth. At this mating, you will receive all your powers and contact from Michael, as he returns to Earth to help insure your destiny.

"There is a maximum and minimum destiny potential for all beings. You and your brother unite in your adult lives; for when you find your brother's rod of power, you also find your father's. Mating with your brother is your maximum destiny potential, as well as his and Earth's. You and Lucien are integral parts of this evolution. You are its roots, and as you balance with your brother, you will sire races of loving souls in balance with their origins.

"When matter is in flux and growing, it must not misalign with the knowledge. You and Lucien must be mated not only to calm the animals, soothe the oceans, and inspire men to record the past; but also to open anew the portals of the future.

"In between Earth incarnations you will return here to your Godfather Tzadkiel, who waits beyond, and will always help you create the maximum of your destiny. He is your guide, and will protect you on Earth and contact you in adult life every time you are to meet your brother; every time Earth needs you; every time you are to realign the planet. This you must do to achieve the future your father and I have envisioned for you.

"For when you have balanced seven great changes and

produced seven new root races of Man with their hearts in harmony with the Light, then you will have enriched the evolution of this planet, and will approach a new crossroads in your own evolution. Even with your heritage and destiny potential, the outcome of the evolution is your own responsibility. Even the best formulated concepts can go awry, as Luciel so aptly proves. You must tread your Path on Earth with your brother, or both of you will lose this maximum potential, as will Earth. Every being, rock, insect, and facet of light and darkness of Earth are your future. When you feel every part of this, and give this feeling to Lucien, you surround the whole planet in the Great Light and complete the cycle's growth potential: then new crossroads of the cosmos will open.

"We of the Light attain constant energy in motion, in balance. Constant energy in movement and change, but always in harmony with the center. Light always returns to its point of origin, augmented by all the other light it has vibrated past, and through. Light that cannot return to the center burns into raw energy in the abyss.

"There is always a new assignment in evolution: a New Birth; a New Beginning; when one completes the cycles in process, and returns them to the center.

"All beings of Light are involved with the evolution of the Cosmos, with the evolution of life. Life is growth, change, death, and rebirth. Rebirth is the whole moving forward in alignment with the center: with the essence of Light; the Light that evolution strives to spread through the universe; the Light that permeates all levels and all worlds. This Light is for all worlds. This Light is for all life to tap: even in the darkness; even in the abyss.

"There are beings that glorify their own egos or selves. They have disassociated themselves from the whole, and though their energy seems potent, it will only burst into the blackness.

"The Power of Light exists as the whole. This force is the basis of all life and the continuance of form. Life is where light grows. Darkness is nothingness where unbalanced energies and unbalanced life forms fracture and burn out as shooting stars; their energy to be reused, but without the self-identity they glorified. Rebirth exists for all energies, but only those centered in the Light who give their identity to the whole, have the consciousness of the whole and the consciousness of self. Only aligned energies maintain self-identity in rebirth.

"Evolved life forms come to planets to balance. They come to mate. They come to align. Mating is cosmic. It is a potent act of Life that transcends all levels. It is the giving of love, which is Light. Cosmic mating produces physical life as planets and species, but its purpose on the spiritual levels is to produce Light. Light is the creative force of the universe: it is the energy of evolution.

"Humanity is a life form capable of achieving great consciousness: it has the ability to differentiate its own ego and develop it. If the Self is in balance with the whole and gives itself consciously to this reunification, the energy produced is a forward thrust which all evolution shares. If the egos are developed, but with no balance for the whole, they create a dissonant flux which must be balanced by higher life forms in order to prevent the dissonance from spreading. For 'as it is above, so it is below': the Earth is a reflection of the heavens, which give it Life. Remember, Life is growth and change, but it must go forward; always forward. The parts of the whole create this forward impetus by extending energies with love and humility to life forms on slower paths, thereby humbling themselves when they gain knowledge of the paths above them. Your path to love lies in the cosmic mating of the parts of your whole; then your light will realign your planet, as well as yourself.

"Never be afraid of your brother, for he is the other half of your whole. You are the key to his realignment, for Luciel plants seeds of great selfishness in him, and sates him with the fleeting but burning pleasure of unbalance. In his essence, he can never deny you, as you must not deny him; for it is only in the awareness and realignment of your separate parts that the whole can be balanced, and Earth progress to wholeness.

"I will not see you again till you complete your Earth cycles. I, a Mother of races and galaxies, travel many universes, engaged in expanding energies that your consciousness cannot yet conceive. Remember, I took physical form to beget you, and there is always a place in my heart open to you. Look always to the Light my daughter: it is your future and your comfort. Give this Light to your brother when you mate, and together you help Earth achieve maximum destiny potential. When Earth's energies are balanced and centered in this Light, you will have illuminated the new paths of your evolution, and you and Lucien will return to me.

"Tzadkiel will be your Godfather and guardian: trust him for guidance. Remember my love, for this love provides a direct channel from my essence to yours. Picture a golden chalice overflowing with molten moonbeams, exploding into shafts of golden light; then you'll make contact with my spirit.

"The future glows in glory for all energies of the Light. So it is ordained, and shall be orchestrated. We will meet again in victory."

III

"Well, that's some video," Evelyn said to the old man as the vision ended.

"Video is a good concept for you. It is a type of video. All life has videos: they are electrical energy patterns that have passed in proximity to each other and thereby interacted. All Life has energy fields that are its own record of existence; and that includes what is seen, as well as what is acted out through all of its evolutions. Those with developed mind powers can read all these videos: from rocks, planets, trees, and Man. You have energy patterns in your brain of all you have witnessed and accomplished throughout your individual evolutions. Sometimes, the connections for humans are weak, and they cannot read their own patterns of each of these. Those beings with mind development can read not only their own patterns, past and future, but can tap into and read the videos of all other life forms and energies. Remember, even form is pure energy, but vibrating at a slower rate, and in achieving form some lose sight of the essence. Returning the physical form to energy awareness is the goal of your evolution. You are Mariella, and I am your Godfather, Tzadkiel." He smiled, and then laughed at her expression.

"I am Evelyn, and this place is the twilight zone. That vision has nothing to do with me. You might be Tzadkiel, but I'm not Mariella. How do I know you didn't tap into the energy pattern of someone else's past?" Evelyn asked appearing agitated.

"It is your past and your energy patterns. The mirror triggered the awareness of your patterns, and they are emerging through your consciousness. You are Mariella, and you must find your brother, Lucien," Tzadkiel replied.

"My brother, son of Luciel, my mate . . . this is incredible and definitely unbelievable. I'm not a naive pleasure-seeking fool who needs his ego inflated. I have no need of a mate. This whole thing is a sham and facade. There is no path to fulfillment here; only sexual satiation, which is not fulfilling, but depleting," Evelyn cried.

"Instead of the cup half full, it is half empty here. You are my Goddaughter: A Princess of Light, and you cannot deny or avoid your destiny. You are an adult, and it is time to find your brother, your mate, and surround him in love; in Light."

"You've come to the wrong generation, Tzadkiel. All that wasted energy in search of love went out years ago. Today we know that love is an illusion, another crutch for those who cannot stand on their own. I've lived 35 years independently and happily, not wasting energy searching for illusions. I've had many fulfilling moments, and I've had them alone." She recited the words steadily and flawlessly, as if she repeated them frequently.

"Fulfilling, no. You will understand the meaning soon, and love will come too. You have been living in the shadow of your reality, as is part of your birthright. Your inner self has been protected by keeping even you unaware of it. This is—and has been—to protect you from Luciel, for he would attempt to prevent your mating with Lucien."

"Mating? For God's sake, I've just been thrown into advanced metaphysics, and you bring it down to sex. Don't tell me that's the height of your spirituality? Even I can sense the hollowness here in this place, and there certainly is plenty of mating going on."

"No, Mariella, there is no *mating* here; but soon you will

be able to differentiate between the two. Sex itself can be very animalistic, for it is the primal urge of physical creation; but the primal urge of cosmic creation is *mating*: two parts of the whole, uniting in all spheres at the same time, grounded by form-creation.

"The aligned sexual act is also a spiritual act. When the parts of a whole unite, the energy created is centered, yet vast as the cosmos, spewn forth in splendor as it transverses the universes to return to the point of issuance. When two parts of an enlightened whole mate, it results in the creation of worlds, of galaxies, and love. This creation of Light will span the universe when you mate with Lucien, and it will heal the unbalanced surges of Earth's energy fields.

"The children you two will produce are not the only purpose of your mating. Children of aligned mating are born with the Light of love around them, but the other result is the Light of love surrounding Earth for all of its people, to and for all beings on all levels of mind and spirit to tap into. It is a rebalance of form and energy, that we share as a recircuiting of creation. Creation is born out of love." Tzadkiel smiled again.

"Sure Tzadkiel, I'm not only to find my brother, but to save this planet, I've got to have sex with him, and often, right? After all I've seen of unbalances today, we'd have to be very busy. Old man, you are too warped," Evelyn stated in a rebuffing manner.

"When you achieve the balance point, then you can discriminate between warped and worldly. You do not yet believe, but the power which brought you to me has brought you to him. You cannot escape your destiny. You are your Father's and Mother's child, and Light and Balance are your heritage. As each moment passes between us, parts of your aura and mind are vibrating for you to feel again. The shadow is lifting. To meet your Father on Earth, you must greet his Great Staff of Power nestled between the legs of your brother."

"Are all beings so crude, even the higher ones that you claim to be? Is this the height of evolution, the most physical of acts?" she asked passionately.

"That is the secret of all ages, most abused and misunderstood. Sex exists on all levels of existence. 'As above, so below'. Sex can create individual life forms, worlds, and star clusters. Unaligned sex can create vast channels of undirected energy. Without its pattern of direction, energy does not return to its issuance. It whirls out of control towards the abyss, where other unbalanced forces use this energy for negative creations. But for those aligned with Essence, mating is cosmic. It is participating in creation; soaring on energy pulses throughout the universe, and returning to the issuance point enhanced by all other light energy which augments and magnifies the participants. Sex on all levels is a significant stimulus," Tzadkiel said, as he laughed again.

"Well, sex on Earth might be pleasurable, but I can't see its nobility. The other room is filled with sexual stimulation, but there is nothing spiritual about it."

"What happens here is the antithesis of what I am here to teach you; to recircuit your energy patterns and lead you to Lucien. With Lucien, you can reunite your spiritual whole, and when you align in cosmic mating, you can achieve the energy levels you are entitled to. Then the two of you will create and release energy that all those of the Light can share with you," Tzadkiel explained."

"You mean planets and galaxies are created by higher beings having sex?" asked Evelyn in confusion.

"Yes, Cosmic orgasm is organic. How that thought confounds so many on the physical levels! When attaining the true center, you must be reunited with your other spiritual half. This exists for all life when outside the center. Oneness is achieved only in the Essence. Creation is energy produced when two individual parts achieve a whole upon mating, and return to the whole vibrating the reconnection, thereby increasing their consciousness. As all energy of the center is connected by relation, the consciousness of all Life of Light is also heightened. When the two halves of an enlightened whole mate, they give birth to enormous energy fields, which create galaxies and stars.

"As the Ancient One returned to the physical world on Earth, he accentuated a direct link between the physical forms and spiritual energy. All life forms on Earth have the potential to align with the World of Light, and in cosmic mating they recircuit the connection. This is why you must mate with your brother: to recircuit your energy to the whole, and to serve as an example for all on Earth who seek Light. For the Ancient One gave all humans the potential to be Star Children, and in their aligned matings, they can be infused with the energy of the center.

"Luciel does not find Earth worthy of connection to the center. As he has lost his direction and balance, he will not let Earth realign, just as he has chosen not to. He would rather see humans destroy themselves before Earth achieves her return power link. He helps Man create great energy unbalances on Earth, in the hope that Earth would burst its cycle of evolution, and free Lucien from further reincarnation there. But the whole does not permit this. Luciel is a tester, and a builder of Great Change. He helps increase dissonant energy that Earth must expend into earthquakes, volcanoes, floods, and cyclones. This brings the death that must precede rebirth, and is his evolutionary assignment. But he has lost direction by his excessive interference with Earth, as there are many life forms on other planets he ignores in the due course of his assignment. His son's destiny is on Earth, but he believes Earth is inferior in its potential for Lucien. Luciel also lost centering when he felt Earth unworthy of the energy link the Ancient One gave to it.

"This would put a 'hole' in the whole, where, of course, it cannot be. In the whole, all hearts are one, and are also one with the life forms on the physical planes; for the purpose of all Life is to connect with the center. Hence, the reconnection to oneness reflects the growth of all in the growth of the Essence, and the Essence is the sum of all its parts: the sum of all of its individual conscious aspects expanding toward infinity.

"The time is here. You must mate with Lucien to realign your brother, and to realign yourself with the whole. In doing so, you realign the planet Earth. This is the path of your evolution. Free Earth of Luciel's interference and free Lucien. Even in short moments can an evolution be changed," preached Tzadkiel.

"All of this is too much for my consciousness. I'm not an adept; I'm just a simple personality."

"Your simplicity is the other half of your brother's pride. Melded, they are the keys to both your future and your heritage," Tzadkiel replied.

"My heritage? You can't expect me to believe all this. My Mother, some type of Goddess who begets planets as she did me, and my Father, an Archangel? Does that make me an 'Angelette'? A brother who is my complete opposite—if I've understood any of your words—an opposite who instead of hating, I must love; and love with him must include satisfying his lusts. I don't accept this as my future, and I don't accept its relation to my past," Evelyn exclaimed.

"Mariella, you cannot deny your Essence. You have the metaphysics of polarity down pat. You cannot stay in the shadows any longer, for all of your energy connections are starting to recircuit. Knowledge is always a key. Look into the mirror again. Look into the Mirror of the Past."

She looked skeptically at Tzadkiel and the mirror, but the mist reappeared, and the dizziness made her realize how Alice felt upon falling into the looking glass.

IV

The weather was mild, and soft breezes rolled through the meadows and flowers, and whispered through her hair. Her long blond hair billowed out behind her, a golden sail on the wind. Her body tensed as she ran down the hill in exhilaration and abandon. Birds sang and brooks tinkled, and Sylph thought how beautiful life was.

She lay down next to a stream that was an offshoot of one of the four great rivers bisecting Lemuria. She looked at her village beyond, as images ran through her mind of the spiritual and loving people she lived among. Sylph was proud to be a member of Lemuria: the height of Earth civilization, where knowledge and understanding flourished in peace and harmony.

Lemuria was a large tropical island surrounded by the rolling waters of the Great Sea. Mountains at the outer circumference of the island dipped into the waves; and hills, forests, and glades followed into a plateau at the center, wherein stood the city of Mu.

Seven villages spread out beyond the circumference of the central city. The seven villages were communes unto themselves, but also connected to the central city by rivers and roads. Each village, though separate in identity, was also patterned after the Grand Center, Mu.

The villages were also constructed as a reflection of Mu. The houses sat at the circumference of a circle, and in the inner circumference was the school and meeting hall, as well as the hall of crafts and trade. But in the inner core there stood only the holy circle, where people gathered to meditate and pray: a microcosm of the Grand Holy Circle in Mu.

All the structures in the villages were made of wood, with thatched roofs. In the center of each roof was a large open circle, so the Sun or Moon could shine directly in, while rain funneled into a fountain. The buildings of Mu itself were constructed of stone, but they also had the open ceilings. Lemurians wanted to be as close to nature as possible and structures were just forms to these spiritually evolved people. There were no adornments on the buildings, but each village had its own assigned geometric shape and color, and all houses and halls in the village utilized their color and shape in their own designs. Only the Grand City of Mu possessed the combinations of all of the shapes and colors of the seven villages.

Sylph was from the green village. The other six were red, yellow, orange, blue, violet and indigo. The green village was assigned the shape of the cube. Although each village was a whole unto itself, it was also a part of the greater whole of Lemuria. While each had its own Head Master, Elders, and Old One to lead them in meditation and prayer, it was also further magnified by the Grand Masters, Grand Elders, and The Ancient One of the city of Mu.

The principles of Lemuria were love, oneness, respect for each other, and nature. Most importantly for the Ancient of Days design of creation, all members of the community eventually had to be initiated into all of the knowledge and wisdom of all of its parts.

The people of Lemuria represented the five races of Man, with all ages, heights, and sizes being included. Each villager wore a medallion of a golden six pointed star on a metal disc, forged in one of the seven sacred metals which represented the birth villages: iron designated the red village; tin, the blue village; lead, the green village; copper, the indigo village; silver, the violet village; gold, the orange village; and mercury, the yellow village. All of the villages and central core had blended populations, so that the only way to differentiate between the villagers was by the medallions they wore, or the colors of their ceremonial robes which were worn every Full Moon, and on all ceremonial occasions.

Each villager spent an hour every morning at his own holy circle for meditation and prayer. Then, the morning studies began for all those uninitiated students: those who had not yet achieved full development or knowledge. The mode of instruction was different from village to village, as each school was controlled by the individual Head Master, who had free choice to construct the patterns of learning for his villagers. Each Head Master also specialized in parts of the knowledge, so vast was the concept of the whole. He shared that knowledge with his villagers and others in private study.

Every seventh morning on the day of the week assigned to his village, the Head Master had private tutorials with his students to help plan their initiations into the special subjects offered in other villages. Through this arrangement, afternoon classes were completed. One learned a specialized study one at a time until initiation in all seven schools was accomplished. Afternoons were reserved for initiation studies as a tribute to the Great Mother of Seas, who granted Life its differentiation. Every afternoon the rains fell on Lemuria, while villagers studied mental, magical, or physical skills. The Mother of Rains helped to cool physical exertions, or helped to focus those in mental pursuits, while the fountains magically cascaded into differentiated droplets, reuniting in the reflected reservoirs that were at the cores of all buildings.

Each village also had a sacred stone, and a magical note. When the villager received initiation in his own village, he received a note to chant, and a stone to place in the center of his golden six pointed star. Further initiations provided six other magical notes to vibrate, and six other stones to adorn the points of the star. By this system, one could not only see the level of initiation a villager had achieved, but his birth village as well, by simply noting the type of metal disc. The stones and notes were assigned as follows: red village, ruby; the note, "do"; orange village, pearl; the note, "re"; yellow village, diamond; the note, "mi"; green village, emerald; the note, "fa"; blue village, sapphire; the note "so"; violet village, almandine garnet; the note, "la"; and the indigo village, amethyst; the note, "ti."

At full initiations into all seven villages, the Lemurians could choose to live in the Grand City of Mu in order to attend the functions of the whole community and live by the Halls of Wisdom and the Galleries of Music and Art. Or, they could choose to return to their birth village or any of the others.

Full initiates therefore, had free choice of where to live, and what to teach or share, as his own highest contribution to the whole. But even full initiates were to return to a village when they had children. There they must remain to nurture them, or else leave them in the care of a village family. Thus, everyone in the community had a birth village, and potential for development and growth. Everyone was allowed to visit the Grand City anytime, but only full initiates could reside there permanently.

Late afternoons were reserved for the personal choice of work, studies, or pleasure. Sunset brought everyone back to their village for evening prayers in the inner circle: the note of the village was chanted to induce everyone to feel oneness with the whole. The Elder or Headmaster also told a story, or posed a problem that the Lemurians could discuss at home during the evening meals.

At the Full Moon, all seven villages traveled leisurely to Mu by boat or by path, and passed the night in the forests outside of the city communing with nature. Then, they all entered Mu the next morning, and gathered at the Grand Holy

Circle for community prayers. The celebrants wore identical long, silk gowns in the color of their birth village, and formed three circles in the Grand Holy Circle. The outer circumference included those not fully initiated, standing six apart from their fellow villagers in the order of the colors of the prism. The middle circle of the fully initiated also followed the pattern of the colors of the prism, with the inner circle being composed of the Grand Masters and Grand Elders, dressed in white.

Together they surrounded the altar: a solid diamond cube structure, surmounted by a golden six pointed star with a white translucent globe at its apex. Next to the altar, the Ancient One, the founder of Lemuria, prayed, and as he raised his hands, all Lemurians vibrated the magical notes of their villages in the order of the scale, and chanted the other magical notes they were initiated to hear. The Grand Masters and Grand Elders walked solemnly to the altar and individually placed their foreheads to the globe. Upon which they returned to the inner circle. When all returned, the vibrating notes ceased, all looked to the Ancient One. He placed his forehead to the globe and vibrated a word. Only the inner circle could understand it, for the rest of the Lemurians saw only an exchange of light energy between the Ancient One and the globe. Then the members of the inner circle vibrated the word in turn, each using the tones of his birth village. The sound vibrated around the Grand Holy Circle seven times, but only the fully initiated heard the word seven times seven. The uninitiated heard the word only in the tones of their birth village, and those others they had been developed to hear.

Sylph sat at the stream and calmed her thoughts. She had only half listened in class that morning. She was normally a serious student, and her lapses of attention bothered her. Lemurians communicated telepathically, so a loss of attention was a loss of a lesson. The subjects presented that morning were physics and astrology, ones which she had already begun to master, so she was not worried that her present inability to concentrate would affect her overall progress. After all, she was one of the youngest members of the community to have three other stones besides her birth stone on her medallion. She felt anticipation drawing her from concentration. In morning meditation, her village father, Tanin, had asked her to return home before afternoon studies. That was a departure from the pattern: something uncommon for him. Lemurians hummed as they communicated thoughts from mind to mind, so the humming provided a window to the emotions and feelings. Essentially, a multi-level communication resulted. Tanin's humming that morning had described expectancy and sadness. Sylph had not noticed that emotional combination in him before, so she meditated on her beloved Father.

She was proud of him, for he was an educated and gentle man. He wasn't her birth parent, but she had been given into his care and the loving arms of his wife, Zamora. The answer as to her birth parentage was shrouded in mystery, for she did not know if her parents resided in Lemuria or came from other lands. No one would discuss the subject with her, and to Sylph questions of her beginnings were long forgotten. Instead, she remembered the nurturing and loving Tanin and Zamora had provided. They were both fully initiated, but chose to live in the green village in order to raise the child they had been given to love. Tanin was the community's foremost Talisman craftsman, and even after he left Mu to live with Sylph in the green village, most community members made their way to his door. No one else could create the perfect amulet, or alter a medallion with new stones as magically as he. Everyone respected her Father and Mother, and she foremost; her long ago past didn't interest her, for her future now unfolded in tense excitement.

"Hello Father and Mother! What is different today, and so important? I can feel the tension in the air." Sylph hummed in excitement as she rushed in to hug her parents.

Tanin's hum overflowed with love. "You have been the best part of our lives, giving us much joy and growth. Even we could not imagine how wondrous parenting would be. You are a joy, and the best of our dreams are for you. We are most proud of you, daughter. But now your destiny opens, and hidden knowledge unfolds and guides you to your future. You will soon have the answers to questions you wondered about."

"I no longer think of the past. It slides by as each day the sun slides into the horizon. You are all that is important to me of my past," Sylph hummed in awareness and devotion.

"The real past can not be forgotten, and must be understood to be assimilated. Would that we could change destiny and keep you with us. But that would deny your maximum potential, and we could not allow that. You were born of Great parents, evolutions farther evolved than our consciousness can fathom. You have a grand destiny to follow, and you do so for yourself and for us, and for all our people. The burden of the growth of Lemuria rests with you. More than this Zamora and I do not know. Still we have loved you child, with our full hearts; and we hope the sum of us rests in your heart. The Grand Master Tzadkiel requests that we bring you to him this Full Moon. We knew someday he would call for you, as he gave you into our care years ago. More knowledge has not been granted us," Tanin replied with reverence and awe. He and Zamora placed many loving images of their past together in Sylph's thoughts.

Sylph's humming was shrill, but her thoughts clear. "Are we to be parted? I sense you are saying goodbye! I do not want to be parted from you!"

"Do not fear daughter. Tzadkiel will now direct your future. He is the highest Grand Master, and you are honored to be so chosen. I too am pained at the thought of parting, and I hope it will not be too long a separation. But we must accept it even if it is painful, for you have a destiny few could imagine." Zamora hugged and cried with Sylph, as Tanin continued. "Dry your eyes both of you. Change is not always pleasant, but is necessary for growth. We all want the maximum potential for you. It is your birthright. Listen! I have a way to rouse smiles. We could leave by canoe and have an extra evening and day to sun and swim, and share our love in the forest glades before the Full Moon tomorrow. Let's be a happy, carefree family again, if only for hours more." Tears also began to fall from his eyes.

"I can see how painful this is for all of us. No more unhappy thoughts. A family picnic is a wonderful idea. I'll send a message to the blue village Head Master, and we can leave immediately. I too refuse to waste a single moment we can share together." Sylph embraced them both, and hummed soothing and loving tones.

V

Sylph, Tanin, and Zamora entered the Grand Holy Circle holding hands and humming of contentment and love shared. Sylph joined the outer circle while her parents joined the second circle of full initiates. Sylph looked past her parents to the inner circle, and saw the Grand Master Tzadkiel smiling at her. He placed visions in her consciousness of her Mother, Marah and her Father, Michael. The chanting started as Sylph absorbed her past while vibrating the note of her birth village, and the others she received on initiations, and her destiny unfolded in her mind.

The inner circle of Grand Masters and Grand Elders walked one at a time to the altar and reverently placed their foreheads on the globe. The chanting grew ever stronger as the Ancient One approached it. The chanting passed into poised silence as he placed his forehead on the globe and received the word. Then he traveled the circumference of the circle, chanting and vibrating the word. The inner circle chanted the word, with the middle and outer circles joining. The tones reverberated until the air was filled with resonating sounds of reverence and awe.

The Ancient One raised his hands. Silence fell as he placed in their minds and hearts the importance of the message to come. Tzadkiel joined the Holy One and turned the circle, directing thoughts to all of them while reverently chanting the word.

"People of Lemuria. You have created a peaceful and loving world where the spirit is strong, and one in which your minds are connected to the Ancient of Days loving concept of creation. You have developed your consciousness to love this planet and each other in an affirmation of the love of creation which granted you Life. You are the positive and true force of Light, and have lived here in peace and isolation from the greed, lust, and hate which exists in the peoples of the Outlands. But the Great Earth Change approaches; it is a time of great flux for all of you also. The Mountain of Fire will blow most of this island apart before the end of the next Full Moon. Few will survive if they remain here. Also, an army of Outlanders approach; and there is the key to your great change, Lemurians. The other side of the lesson you have achieved in separateness and growth of the individual ego must now be sacrificed to the whole; that is now larger than before, and shared for the growth of evolution.

"Earth has both night and day, dark and light, negative and positive: as the Earth is a microcosm of the Heavens. Force and form are both parts of creation, and must be balanced in order to achieve harmony and alignment with the cosmos. You have learned to transmute and sublimate your energy, and now you must use your potent positive energy to balance the negative forces now arriving as the preordained destiny of Earth's evolution.

"The Outlanders come with hate in their hearts and war on their minds: this you must transmute and balance. This is the lesson of polarity. Love and hate are not only opposites, but are the complements of each other. Two opposing forces find expression and harmony in balance; they are the total of the two individual parts, and more by the energy created in the alignment. Either one absent or present in unequal proportions would destroy the balance, and flush equilibrium out of this evolution. One without the other is an opposite. Together, they are complements. Only balance perches polarity; so the opposing forces reach close enough to trigger the natural desire to exchange and elevate energy surmounting the individual force; repelling its counterpart.

"Man will know love and hate throughout the eons. You are the givers of Love and Light, but your knowledge of both must encompass the negative side as represented by hate, or your understanding is limited and opposed to creation. Siding with one part or the other brings growth of the ego, but the period of Great Change brings the bridge that spans the gulf between them. Then you can receive the negative flow and transmute it, returning the flow which initiates the growth and expansion of both forms of energy. Separateness has precipitated the unbalances now fluxing on Earth, and all sources of energy must realign so the pendulum of polarity balances in poise; not wildly swing from one acute angle to its opposite extreme.

"You must not approach the negative forces with your latent negative side. That would be a negative-negative energy and that is what shall be named "Evil," but misunderstood by Man. Negative energy itself is not evil, but the complement to the positive. The negative and positive must meet and blend in equal proportions, or the unbalance will destroy the aim of growth, thus minimizing the potential for Earth and its Children of Light. Positive-positive unbalances are also a threat to aligned growth. The cup must fill gently and the overflow controlled, or it will totter on its axis and fall, flooding to either side.

"You are Lemurians, and have recognized the waste of materialism. You are the spiritual seeds of evolved energy, but you must grow with the Earth to achieve full potential. You must transmute the physical world and the people who live over the edge of darkness. Evil, envy, murder, and greed must be changed. You must transmute them, and increase their sharing the positive, not expending additional negative power from yourselves to fester and undermine evolution. Rather, you must transmute negative energy by infusing it with the Light. In reflection, you must see that all parts of this evolution, all energy here, is a part of each of us to share together as the parts of our combined whole. All energy is internal as well as external, and we cannot sever the connections.

"Hating them for their ignorance does not bring understanding. They hate you because you are different. You must love them for their differences and assimilate every facet of life open to you. Don't hate them for the mirrors they shine on the latent negative energy you house, for they hate you also for the reflections you pose. You must exchange the energy in order to transmute it, and connect the proper electrical, magnetic, and magical energy, so this flow balances all parts of this whole.

"Remember: what you have developed in separateness, you must now sacrifice for the whole. You are not the enemies of the peoples approaching, but their brothers and their mates. You must face them with love and understanding. Your minds and souls are strong enough to engulf their energy and change them. They will not hurt you if you use mind control and meld, instead of repelling. All must leave Lemuria together or die alone, for the old makes way for the new. The death of Lemuria is the birth of a new evolution on Earth. You are the seed races of Light, born of energy brought to Earth to define it and add to its glorious future. You have the potential at this Great Change to make a great change within yourselves. That is the grand concept of evolution; to create the change of energy within yourselves to precipitate a microcosm of creation. Then the Children of Earth can travel the paths of evolution with their eyes and hearts open; sharing, transmuting, and exchanging all energy of the cosmos.

"The new dawn rises. Gather your possessions and say goodbye to this land that has granted you peace, beauty, and sustenance. Ships are waiting at the shore. Your new future will unfold in new lands, determined by your free will and choice. Make use of the gifts given to you, or you waste energy, instead of recharging and expanding it. Those of you with families: do not isolate yourselves again. Find those among the Outlanders who could be part of your new communes. Those of you unmated have the greatest potential of all, for your polar mates approach. If this be the case, do not waste the growth potential now available. This is a gift of your maximum destiny. Go now in peace and understanding. Hold to your minds the thoughts you have received today, and remember the word received in this last Holy Day of Mu. The word is CREATION."

The Lemurians filed out of the Grand Holy Circle in thoughtful silence. Sylph approached Tzadkiel. "Thank you for the knowledge, Godfather. Thank you also for the visions of my past. It is good to see you and feel the love you surround me with." Sylph looked into his eyes and presented him with her favorite memory of him.

"Your tone does not agree with your thoughts. I sense desolation and despair behind your happiness." Tzadkiel told her.

"You have shown that my beautiful Lemuria is doomed and her people must scatter to the ends of the Earth. Don't worry, I understood the lesson. I see the old must make way for the new, but change is not always desired or easily accepted." Sylph realized the comprehension of evolution.

"Energy patterns are resistant to change; but if not altered, become static even at high rates of vibration. Change first arrives with the death of the old. But the death of the old heralds the birth of the new: one creating the stimulant energy required to balance and evolve the existing energy patterns that permit the greater growth of all conscious energy. That is the aim of evolution and the continuance of creation; where all parts of the whole have awareness of the whole even in their re-separation into individual parts. Lucien, your brother, The Prince, approaches. He is your cosmic mate, infinitely rarer than a polar mate. Do you sense what this means?" Tzadkiel's humming was tinged with anticipation of her reply.

"I suppose my mind accepts all the lessons of today, but my heart does not. I do not wish to desire my brother. He is too possessive and dominant. There must be someone here better suited for him. Perhaps a daughter of one of the Grand Masters." Sylph tried to convince herself and Tzadkiel.

"Lucien is your destined cosmic mate. He is the Prince, and you his Princess. Many may desire him, but only you can balance him, and only he can truly balance you. Spirit has the need of matter. Mating is the natural instinct of all Life, from avatars to ants: that is the stimulus and drive of creation. You are both direct descendants of enlightened beings who gave you, their children, this gift of physical life and the Kingdom of Earth.

You and Lucien together were given the keys to this kingdom; to be caring and creative caretakers of all Life here on Earth. You must use your combined energy to balance your birth planet, nature, and your partners men. The Kingdom of Earth has enough self anointed kings who, in self righteous reflection, take and make what they want. They do not see that there is a connection to the consequences of their actions and that each of us is ultimately responsible for all of us. You and Lucien must mate, or add to this irresponsible buildup of unbalances. You must seek maximum potential together. Earth's maximum potential for all is greatly determined by the few. You two are a force of the few.

"Are not your inner senses opening? Do you not understand the power you will generate by this fusion? This destiny is for yourself, the people here you love, and the planet you help to evolve. Remember: the active force reacts on the passive one, fills it with energy, and is spent. The other, on receiving the energy, overflows and conducts the overflow back to the initiator, who then refills with the new transmuted energy and reinitiates the spiral. Cosmic mating is an exchange of actions and reactions of roles and poles in the ebb and flow of creating cosmic energy and life." Tzadkiel filled Sylph with images and knowledge, his gentle tones opening her awareness and revitalized her respect for the growth.

"Yes, Godfather. I love you, and I do understand. I will love him also, my brother, my mate. Lead me to Lucien, Godfather."

VI

Tzadkiel and Sylph walked out of the Grand Holy Circle. They passed Tanin and Zamora who were waiting for them. Tzadkiel smiled at them and continued on, as Sylph embraced and kissed them. She had to dash to catch up with her Godfather, but turned for a farewell wave to her parents.

"You must look forward now, Sylph. What was behind has already been assimilated." Tzadkiel altered the chains of her thoughts. She looked ahead and saw an army march through the city: fierce men and women fully sheathed in metal, banishing metal swords. At the head of the column rode Lucien, the Prince, garbed only in a loin cloth. He had dark eyes and hair; his bronze skin glowed with rippling muscles. The marauders approached the Lemurians, who smiled and hummed to them. As they drew their swords and looked at their victims, they were mentally persuaded to resheath their weapons. Tzadkiel and Sylph stood by the Hall of Music and watched Lucien and his General alight near them. Sylph could see their eyes as they walked toward and then past them. The Prince's eyes were clear and capricious, shining with intelligence; but the General's were cruel and feral, riddled with malice.

"Tell them to lower their weapons. The people are not opposing us and pose no threat. Have them fan out and investigate. I'm anxious to learn of the great treasures rumored to be hidden in Mu. So far, it seems like a primitive farming colony. But legends don't lie: there is usually truth hidden in them." Lucien looked around at the buildings as the General walked over to some of his men. He listened to them, gave his orders, and returned to the Prince.

"There seems to be no palace, my lord. All the buildings here are simple structures. We have seen little evidence of gold and jewels, except for these medallions." The General handed two medallions to Lucien, and steered him into the elliptical building in front of them. "Why don't you stay here my lord?"

They entered the building. Lucien was enthralled by the sculptures, paintings, and carvings, that filled the Grand Halls of Art. "These are not simple people. This art is incredible. My Father would adore this collection: quite electrifying and visionary. Look at those stone carvings, General." The General looked askance at Lucien, who walked through the long halls and continued. "These people have much to tell. This art is worth a fortune. Don't look puzzled. I'm not crazy; not here on primitive Earth, but in other galaxies this collection would create quite a stir. Let me see those medallions." He stroked them and placed each to his forehead. "Go now, my friend. I have much to think about, and I want some more answers on the Lemurians." Lucien talked, but his mind was now enthused with a puzzle, and the exercise of his curiosity was one of his greater pleasures. Wealth meant little to the son of Luciel, whose father honored all his wishes and invented new ones for him. Lucien loved to think, and mysteries were more exciting to him than gold and jewels. Still, his people had to have the rewards they sought. He would find the keys to this community, and learn of the Lemurians who live in primitive structures, and yet could create cosmic art.

The General again passed Tzadkiel and Sylph. This time he stopped and looked at Tzadkiel, who returned a smile and mesmerized his mind. The General staggered away in confusion as Tzadkiel smiled at Sylph and pointed. "You always save that special smile for me Godfather, when you have brought me to my brother and freed yourself from Earth." Sylph hummed of regret.

"We don't have much time physically together on Earth, but I am always protecting and loving you. Out of your Earth incarnations, we spend much time together. You are definitely one of the special relationships of my life. That is why I gladly come to the dense worlds of form to protect and guide you through the crossroads of your destiny. Lucien's Father is forever trying to prevent your mating. He devotes much energy in searching for you, before the union solidifies both of your powers, and reopens channels which temporarily estranges Luciel from you. On mating, Lucien will love you also in equal intensity as is his love for his Father. Luciel could never stand to share anything. What Luciel wants, he takes and covets for himself. That is an overcharge of his potent negative energy. That is part of the folly he gives to his son. You give Lucien the birthright of his Mother. Also, as pleasure lovers, neither can deny that the son's greatest ecstasy lies in you. Luciel can't redirect that, and once the bond is made, he will not fight your Earth union, for he would never take passion away from his son.

"Don't look disheartened. If you look deeply into the essence of your being, you will see that you choose him freely, and will continue to do so over many lifetimes. Some people are lucky to find a polar mate during form incarnation, but few are evolved enough to have cosmic mates. And of those, few find them in form incarnation.

"Lucien is the center of all your dreams, as you are the core and definition and focus of his. He takes you to the vast outer limits he dominates, and you take all the energy you encounter and infuse it with direction through focus such that it returns to the center. That new energy becomes your children, as well as the physical ones your body will create. This destiny is only possible with you two together. Has not awareness reached you yet?" Tzadkiel asked in surprise, his weak humming showing the depletion of his physical energies.

"Go home, Godfather. Thank you for caring and loving. I can see you are ready to depart your weakening Earth form. It must be quite a task to fit all of your vast spirals of energy into so small a form. I will mate with my brother. It is my choice, and I reaffirm it. I would not disappoint you or take the keys from the kingdom. My destiny and pleasures await. Goodbye my love." Sylph kissed Tzadkiel on his eyelids and forehead, and his form disappeared. Sylph entered the Grand Halls of Art and stood behind a statue listening to Lucien and his General.

"There seems to be no great wealth here Lord. The medallions have gems and metals on them, but there are not that many medallions; only one for each villager, and that is the only jewelry they wear. There are also these small golden sheets inscribed with strange shapes which we found in another hall. That is the sum of what we have found. They are simple people, and cannot even communicate. Instead, they hum and chant some type of gibberish," the General admitted in disappointment.

"They are rich in knowledge, General. Those sheets are their books. All the geometric shapes are sentences and concepts. That it's a language which embodies such concepts is not a simple accomplishment. They are a spiritual people, and have little use for the pleasures of the physical world. But look at the medallions. The diamonds, gold, and wealth are here; I'm sure of that. The Lemurians never tapped their wealth; it's still waiting for us in their hills and mountains. We'll just have to work harder for it. Tell the others not to waste their time in the city. They must spread out over Lemuria and discover the mines. "Lucien pacified the General and dismissed him. Lucien wanted them to have their rewards, but his were here. He was memorizing every piece of art, and would send the impressions to his father who would recreate the thoughts back into the matter they described. He heard music resounding through the halls to which the sculptures and carvings seemed to revolve.

Then he saw Sylph dancing toward him. Lucien turned his full attention to her, and saw her nakedness beneath the silken veils. She was tall, thin, and willowy, her blond hair swaying as rhythmically and hypnotically as her body. He was entranced. His mouth was moving; no sound appeared, but perspiration broke out on his upper lip and chest.

As before in past lives, when confronted with her sexuality, he lost control. There was a green mist before his eyes; and Sylph. His stare became hypnotizing, and before she could break the mind meld, or her eyes from his, he had her in his embrace.

With a groan that vibrated through the room, he kissed her and drowned in the sensations. He tried to settle and soothe her with one hand, as the other caressed her still dancing body. He was inflamed, and pushed her to the floor and mounted her. The music and their bodies moved to a crescendo of sensations. They soared through the cosmos in seconds, to return to climax in Earth form where they both lay, panting and entwined.

"Well, my brother. Your physical prowess is never over stated. And so diversified. I love the way you make love, Lucien." Sylph admitted to him and herself.

"So you can speak, my sister."

"Of course I can speak. If you weren't so overly physical, you would have noticed me communicating directly to your mind. Humming reveals the emotional content of the concepts: multi-facet communication." Sylph replied in satisfaction.

"Our physical sharing extends to awareness. I know in your secret thoughts you see yourself as the positive sacrifice to my negative desires. Don't take offense. You'll have to get used to my teasing personality. After all, we're to be together for long spans of Earth time. I can share in your mental powers, as you can pleasure yourself with my physical ones."

Lucien started to caress her again.

"If you have full awareness, how come you don't see how little time we have?"

"How little time is left to Lemuria I now know also, but our time together is unlimited, and we have plenty of cosmic mating to look forward to. I'm eagerly awaiting more." He soothed her with his voice and hands." I will lead us to the Outlands. All in good time beloved." The General stomped in, and Lucien rolled over, sat up, and looked into the General's malicious grin. "You have to practice your smiles, General. They don't suit you, yet. Anyway, don't look so smug. If you must know, she seduced me." Lucien teased again.

"Seduced you! Why you conceited fool! All you take for seduction is part or all of the female anatomy. Why you . . ." Lucien interrupted, sent her a smile that melted her anger, and then turned to the General. "I can see the General has little interest or patience in our games. I have learned General, that before the next Full Moon the volcanoes of Lemuria will erupt, and earthquakes will blow apart this island. You must see that everyone leaves before then. There are plenty of ships available at the coast. Our people may take whomever and whatever they find with them, but they must leave this place and return to the Outlands," Lucien replied in conviction.

"How can you be so sure, my Prince? I don't see any evidence of volcanoes or earthquakes."

"Trust in my knowledge, my friend. Remember, it was my knowledge which designed the ships that brought us here. Trust that knowledge again, and direct the others to escape. They have time to accumulate supplies and their rewards. These are my orders, for few of those who remain will survive. If you seek survival, you must journey back across the Great Sea. I go myself, General." Lucien rose and patted him on the back. The General was startled, but pleased. "Do you go alone, my Prince? I will be honored to accompany you."

"No, General, that was a slip of my tongue. I am alone no

longer. I have my sister, Mariella, to share my journey. Smile a hello to the General, dear. I'm sure we'll meet again in the Outlands, but for now it's goodbye. Remember, you must all leave before the next full Moon," Lucien reminded again.

"Goodbye for now, my Prince and you too, my Princess. I will find you in the Outlands; that is a fact I will stake my life on. I will leave you alone now." The General replied and retreated, still smiling.

Lucien lay down again atop his sister. "There is one consciousness between us now, and we become one being while mating. How the pleasures I find with you, Mariella, make all other pleasures pale in comparison. There is no way to compare simple physical sex with cosmic mating. And I love our destined way of meeting. How my rod of power fills your cup of creation. A penetrating and probing presentation. I do like how you say hello, sister. Let's say hello again."

VII

Sylph and Lucien climbed down the hidden path on the steep, craggy mountain to alight at a small dock overlooking a lagoon whose waters reflected the sleek elegance of the masts and rigging of a sailboat. "Here's my other beautiful lady, Mariella. This is my beloved ketch, 'Caprice'. I have sailed her on many oceans in many galaxies. Thank you again, Father. He's the best dispatcher in the galaxies; he can move matter around the universe, and it always arrives in perfect condition. Never underestimate my Father. There are few Archangels who equal his powers with matter." Lucien caressed the hull and the rigging of his ship. "She is always eager for new waters, my Caprice. And so am I."

On top of the mast were mounted two large crystal prisms, which started to pulsate and glow. "What is that, Lucien?" Mariella watched in fascination. Lucien looked up at the mast, and down to the instrument panel in the cockpit. "They're my power crystals, vibrating. They power the electrical systems on Caprice, and a turbine engine when she is lacking wind, but I have not turned on the power switch. One of our parents is coming. "Lucien saw the light pour down from the crystals to surround Mariella in bright beams, and then the light surrounded him also. He felt the charges of positive energy pulsate through him, and he knew it was Michael.

"That's a beautiful ship you have there, Lucien. I admit you always take my daughter travelling in style," Michael answered, as he took denser form and hugged his daughter.

"Father!" Mariella gushed as she hugged him fiercely. "I was waiting and hoping to see you."

"And I am pleased to see you, my daughter. You look wonderful. This has been a loving incarnation for you. Lemuria is a paradise of Earth not to be equaled again for many thousands of years. I hope the seeds of its light are deep within you."

"I assimilated them also on our mating." Lucien interjected, now having both their attention. "As firmly planted as is my seed. We will go to the Outlands and establish a family and community in harmony and balance with our Kingdom Earth. I find the paths of our destiny multiplying into infinity, but my future and my greatest pleasures all stem from such a small, tight space," Lucien teased.

"There you go again Lucien, differentiating my separate parts. How many times must I express my desire for you to relate to the whole of me, not just my anatomy," Mariella retorted.

"Certainly my darling. I do love the whole of you, but that doesn't diminish the delicious desire to savor and suckle your adorable parts." Lucien laughed and kissed her.

"Well children. I can see it is time for your sea voyage. I will meet you in the Outlands." Michael took both their hands, and raised them to his forehead. He noticed Mariella's look of longing. "Do not fret, daughter. I will see you soon. Aren't I always here to help with Earth Changes and Man?

"I want to absorb as much of this Garden of Life as I can. Lemuria forever will rate in Earth history as the most spiritual of societies, and this planet won't reattain that cosmic concentration of evolved energies for eons to come. Go and enjoy your reunion alone. I will meet you in your future. Remember I love you both." Michael kissed Mariella on her forehead, and untied the lines. Lucien waved, raised sails, and they soared away.

Michael watched them depart and turned to see Luciel skulking out from behind a boulder, angry and preoccupied. "Why were you hiding, my brother? Didn't you want the children to see you?" Michael faced him but neither embraced the other.

"And let Lucien see how angry I am? Never. I always avoid alienating him with personal anger. He is my son, an I must live with his choices so I can continue to hold his trust and council him. Persuasion is more practical than anger. He has found cosmic mating with your daughter and is momentarily distracted. I won't bother him now with my disappointments. Earth time is but seconds in eternity.

"Soon he will return to me in satiation and elation, and be most accessible to my persuading beliefs. I save my anger for you, my righteous half brother. You don't see the waste of their evolutions here on inferior Earth. I'll also reserve some anger for Man.

"Man is hopeless. He is not capable of handling his affairs, much less balancing the energy of either of us. He distorts the images he has of both of us to favor one over the other in periods of unleashed electromagnetic unbalances. This is the mess you seem to relish by asking my son and your daughter to balance it. I do not understand your adherence to this wasted lesson. Our children will work for this kingdom that will be destroyed my Man. Man will blast his planet out of evolution." Luciel's rage resounded through the mountains.

"I appreciate your concern for the children's welfare, but hard work and dedication never hurt them. Challenges raise their expectations and cancel limitations. They will succeed in reuniting the Spiritual Kingdom of Earth to its physical counterpart, though this will take many changes and many incarnations. They have chosen to balance now and in the future. You cannot change the lessons they have elected," Michael replied, trying to keep the annoyance he felt from his voice.

"You and Marah elected the lessons for the children. I was

not consulted. You gave them the Kingdom of Men; Man is not worthy of this attention or help, and he cannot be an equal partner in Earth's evolution. He cannot help our children, or the Son of the Ancient Of Days. Man will destroy this kingdom, distort the children's destiny, and abort the evolution of this planet," Luciel railed.

"Our children together are the hope of form on Earth; they walk the planet among the people as brothers and sisters. They bring harmony, and define the patterns for Man and themselves. They are all partners, and all dependent on each other. As the Son of the Ancient Of Days has shown, they are all equal partners of the whole that can be Earth's evolved destiny: equal partners and laborers in the future of this evolving whole. Save your defiance and depression for other planets: leave this one and the children alone. They can not attain full potential if this planet and Man do not. How can you tamper with their future?" Michael protested and persuaded.

"Because tampering is the stimulus which precedes transmutation. It is my assigned purpose to bring the stimulation of forces to redefine the forms. That is also a part of cosmic creation, and the development of deserved destiny. Man will soon descend from connected spiritual awareness to steep himself in the physical world. He will revel at the potency of my energy, and reel from the realization of it, for he will never learn to balance or control energy. Energy just dissipates through him, to loose its individual identity. It is not transmuted into a controlled new pattern, but rather, becomes a flux of unbalances in this wrecked whole," Luciel replied in smug satisfaction.

"I agree, brother, that you have a misunderstood role in evolution; a hard path to follow. But Man of Earth is very like you, Luciel. You can easily describe their blind rages and rash judgments, for you know them well. You have many traits in common, including an over emphasis on the physical forms themselves, not on the forces motivating them. I love to hear your dissertation on the whole: it makes no sense when you seek to disregard transmutation and connection to the whole, or any part of it to yourself. Maybe that is why you belittle men for their imperfections. Maybe they mirror an uncomfortable reflection to you also; of your concentration on the separate parts, instead of seeing the potential in uniting energy.

"Control takes concentration as well as patience. I have hopes for Man and you also, on that score. Man will Earth himself to the physical worlds, but he will revolve back to spiritual awareness and recircuit the forces to the forms. Man of the future will learn to transmute your forces Luciel, as well as mine. I hope you too will wish to realign with our whole, and transmute your refined energy for all of us to share. I have faith in Man and in you Luciel, my whole brother: half is simply a concept of your separation.

"You must acquire patience and understanding. Our children have joined again in cosmic mating. The cycles of their combined destinies on Earth remain unbroken. This new cycle for them has just begun. I have made myself a part of this future here. You could also, my brother," Michael explained, feeling visions of light and balance flowing through his being.

"Share imperfection! Take tiny steps when I can soar towards galaxies? No thanks. I'll leave the children and Earth under your care!

"But be prepared, Michael. The next incarnation will break the cycle, for it will not be so easy to mate them again. I will teach Lucien how to overpower this kingdom, and how to avoid your willful daughter. Remember: for you my brother, it is how you play the game; but for me, it is the sheer pleasure of playing and winning, with no rules applying." Luciel's maniacal laugh faded as he departed.

VIII

A woman stood on the shore of a dark choppy sea. The wind whipped her body and her clothes, as the waters boiled, her hair stung her face as the wet and wild strands wrapped around her.

A metal cylindrical ship emerged from the waters and glided to the small dock. She watched the Boatman alight. Never had she seen a man like this: he was part man and part fish, with enormous unblinking eyes, a bulging mouth, and no neck: only a type of gills atop the normal torso. His skin was the same metallic gray as the shell of the ship, but his was scaled, while the ship's was smooth. "Are you Zallah?" he asked.

"Yes," she answered.

"Come aboard. Tzadkiel summons you. I will take you to Atlantis."

The inside of the ship was filled with instruments she had never seen before. The red and green glow they emitted made her weary, and giving in to the tensions, she cringed with claustrophobia.

She moved to the one large window and saw they were travelling through a glass tunnel under the water at amazing speeds.

She saw the bow of the ship was constructed of crystals and lenses. The light it received from the sun was amplified by the glass, and used to power the ship.

This increased her alarm and fear of Atlantis, for she was raised among simple people who lived with no such power or tools, simply off the land and forest. The people of Atlantis were rumored to be superior but cruel, as they came to the Outlands and enslaved the peasants.

The time passed painfully slow as all her fears surfaced. Who was this Tzadkiel who claimed to be her Godfather; and why summon her to Atlantis, the Forbidden City, when she had a serene and peaceful life in the forest, and a communion with nature? What would these people be like: cruel, or intelligent? What would they look like? Would they be fish-like, as the Captain?

The ship reemerged from the water and landed at a small dock at the edge of a forest. But this forest was screeching and ominous, and felt unnatural. They both alit, the Captain saluting an old man in white robes. He had gentle and wise sparkling eyes, his body and face similar to hers, yet his aura was regal, and he calmed her by his smile. "I am Tzadkiel, your Godfather. Welcome to Atlantis. Your destiny awaits you."

"I have answered your summons Tzadkiel, but I am happy with the destiny I have. I did not want to come here, but I felt an unexplained responsibility to see you. Why didn't you come to me in the forest? If you're my Godfather, why have you deserted me all these years?"

"I have never deserted you, Mariella. I have been your Godfather for many eons, but on Earth I did not make contact directly with you while you were a child for your own protection. But I always know what you do, what you feel, and what you must do for your future," said Tzadkiel, as his eyes sparkled with feeling.

"Yes, I believe you. I know now you are my Godfather, for you have released strong emotions in me that I have never felt before. Yet, I have never felt in more danger. What is wrong with this place?"

"Atlantis is a magnificent continent surrounded by water and ringed by a dense forest. This forest is now in negation of its natural essence: it is teaming with a negative energy that was generated by dark magicians to keep people from leaving the continent with their minds intact; and to kill people from other lands who made it over the churning waters, thus preventing their further penetration toward the city which lies in the center of this island. Only those who have knowledge of the Words of Power can subdue this strident energy and travel safely," answered Tzadkiel, while leading her to two beautiful unicorns. "Come, let us ride and quickly leave the dark forest."

"White Unicorns! I thought they were mythical beasts!"

"All forms conceived in thought are capable of taking physical form. There are many forms of beings in Atlantis that will amaze and astound you. This is an advanced technological society. The Genetic Institute of Atlantis can bring anything they or you can imagine into living form. But even that is outdone by the offspring of these forms, inbreeding among themselves. Diversity is growth when reassimilated to its roots; but none can achieve that at the speeds of forward thrusts that are developed here. You will see many speed ships here: those of the water, the air, and the land. In this age of advanced technology with unbalanced complexities, I prefer to demonstrate simplicity. The Unicorns provide a balanced beauty, and a fast and comfortable means of travel which grounds me to Earth," said Tzadkiel as he smiled.

Outside the dark forest stretched a rain forest, steaming and teaming with species of palms, orchids, monkeys, and parrots indigenous only to Atlantis; all chirping and coexisting in balanced harmony. They travelled the stone paths leading to the city, and passed people travelling on birds larger than the Unicorns, but slower. These birds did not fly, but rather, hopped forward on stilted feet. Air ships, moving at the intense speeds the water ship accomplished, passed the Unicorns. She looked at all of these creations in awe.

Seeing her expression, Tzadkiel elucidated. "Atlantis has been given the power of Light, though it now abuses this gift. Look at the groups of pillars we pass. They are made of crystal, and are erected in groups of three's throughout the land. On top of the left pillar are lenses directed to the Sun or Moon, or whatever star it best aligns with, while the right one is capped with lenses that are directed to the main crystals of the city. The middle pillar connects the two light beams to allow a constant ebb and flow of light energy. Ships and other forms tune their own lenses and crystals to these pillars, which provide them with this potent and practical power. Light energy is a source of travel throughout the cosmos." Tzadkiel pointed to the clusters of three pillars visible around the horizon.

The land was lush and tropical, with rolling hills sparkling from the vibrating light rays, and reflecting the gold paved roads leading directly into the city. The city of Atlantis was visible in the distance as it sat on a mesa, awash with sunlight, and bisected by its four rivers which cascaded into waterfalls and canals that dotted the community. The entire city appeared elevated toward the Sun, giving the appearance of a majestic mountain which had been bisected crossways, to provide a level base for the clusters of polished stones structures built in various geometric shapes. Each structure was adorned with sculptures of studded precious stones, and all were topped with crystals, thus adding a haunting radiance to the overall vision.

As they neared Atlantis, she could see there were two standard heights for all of the buildings: tall, or a small, single story. On the third highest, central level of the city, were two structures only: a pyramid, and·a cube, each with the largest crystals on its summit. In the center of these two buildings was the tallest and only lone pillar of power in Atlantis. All three of these large globes of crystals could be seen vibrating with intense light energy.

As they entered the city, its structural intricacy paled against the complexity and diversity of its inhabitants. The people were of all colors, shapes, and sizes: some were blends of men and animals; some had wings and talons; some tails and manes; and some feathers or scales. No one was more extraordinary than the other, and the diversity seemed appropriate for this unusual place. The city was bathed in pulsing bursts of light, with the people wearing bright colors, testifying to the vibrancy of this civilization. Life didn't just exist here: Atlantis teamed with it. Though these were unfamiliar sights and sensations, Zallah felt gloriously alive: the fear was gone. The Sun felt hot as it penetrated her skin, with each drop of sweat being a reaffirmation of her place in the cycle of life.

"I see Atlantis has started to awaken your senses and your psyche. Soon you will take the path to your promised destiny. Here is my house. Welcome." Tzadkiel led the way into a building of white polished stone of the smaller size.

"I believe in simplicity in all phases," he said. "People believe the higher structures elevate them to higher powers, but only the powers grounded in Earth can achieve the levels they strive for. Remember: the simple can be the most elaborate, and the lowest, the highest. In change there are no contradictions; just recircuits."

The inside of the house was brightly lit, Zallah noticed light entering from prisms in what she had thought were solid walls. The top of the structure was crystal also, shining rays in all colors of refracted light throughout the structure.

"Relax now, Zallah, for soon the energy of your future will engulf you in change for your rebirth. I have brought you here to Atlantis to meet your brother, your mate." Tzadkiel's eyes twinkled.

"My brother; my mate. My consciousness seems to accept that, but how can that be? I know of no brother." Zallah looked at him in confusion.

"He is not only your physical brother of Earth, he is also

your spiritual brother," he replied. You will mate with him to heal Earth.

"Atlantis is the height of this cycle of Earth's evolution. Light was given directly to the people here, with great technology and mind control being some of its accomplishments. But all things must be balanced, and all parts of the whole must be equal: for in Light there is no inferior or superior, just different speeds of the whole. The individuals here developed their Egos and praised their superiority, which negated the path of evolution and created great unbalances where formally there was harmony. The purpose of civilization is not to foster the perfection of individuals, but to balance the forward movement of all parts of the whole, even the densest forms. The inch travelled by all together is farther reaching than the mile transversed by the single Ego.

"There is no perfection, only evolution. Perfection is a false prophecy and a false reward. Many now in Atlantis have lost the purpose of the Essence, and strive for self-glorification. But glory does not exist in the Ego, only in the whole, and in the sacrifice of the Ego to the whole. The people here have abandoned their grounding. They concentrate on one part of their nature to the exclusion of the other parts. There are those of Atlantis with great mind skills, but with no connection to their souls or bodies. There are those here who see perfection in the physical form itself, without relating it to the consciousness that should direct it. Beautiful bodies of all species are only beautiful energy patterns when they love the whole, and see all the differences of form as the growth of beauty. When you deny fragmentation, all are beautiful, and ugly becomes a fallacy. Souls who generate energy without direction from the mind or grounding in the body, have created a forest of darkness they no longer control. Great minds with no sublimation in the spiritual and no grounding in the physical create surges of unbalanced energy that burns out their physical forms, and fractures their forces.

"Negative force travels to the circumference instead of the center. Negative energy is released when Man sees his own Ego as the center, and thinks the purpose of perfection is to develop the Self to the exclusion of the whole. Slavery and cruelty are the products of men who glorify themselves, but the path of perfection only brings darkness. The Light shines more brightly in the aura of a slave, straining and striving for survival, than on a Scientist who makes weapons of destruction; or in the aura of a Magician who commands demons.

"The scientists and magicians have recognized the surges of uncontrolled energy, though they ignore the recircuiting of their Egos which could balance the energy. Instead, they see themselves as being above other life forms and the nature of their planet. In their colossal selfishness and misdirection, they think they can control the forces of evolution and the natural forces of Earth, with which they have wildly experimented with. They think they can realign the energy by blasting a pressure vent open on the other side of the globe. They are constructing a new Great Crystal, larger than the great ones given to them by the balanced beings who gave them the gift of their knowledge. On the next mid-summer's day, they hope to erect and align it with the Sun and all of the other crystals. This they will accomplish, but the new beginning they precipitate will mean death of their misguided energy. Instead, it will initiate the polar changes that will bring rebirth to Earth, but death to Atlantis. You must mate with your brother and leave here together to fulfill your destiny, and realign this rebirth.

"Your brother Lucien is a Prince of Atlantis. Luciel, his father, has put his cousin, Lilleal, here on Earth to develop his son's powers and to keep you from him. She is alert to your existence, but she cannot locate you. She is totally involved in the perfection of beauty of form, and this obsession blinds her to you, for she cannot conceive of higher beings incarnating in what she deems as less than perfect bodies. She knows

Marah's daughter is beautiful in all worlds, but she cannot see the essence where your beauty lies, and will dismiss your unadorned form. This will be her mistake. It will permit you access to Lucien, who must be saved from the edge of total nervous disorder induced by his overindulgence in sex and drugs.

"Unbalanced forms seek extremes for pleasures, for to unbalance one level is to unbalance all. They seek stimulation in cruelty and sadism, requiring drugs and constant sexual satisfaction to feel anything at all. For feeling is a facet of the Essence, and the single Ego without connection to the whole cannot feel with the whole. It is left with grasping the extremes of itself, which are nothings. Sensation of the whole is the pleasure of all Life combinations felt together by all of the life-centered participants.

"A ceremony is performed on the first Full Moon after the cycle of the new year. All the men of power must demonstrate their control over physical nature and their sexual prowess. They will compete for the honor of mating with Lilleal, for she senses the power of mating, but as in all things, she is misdirected. She constantly indulges in sex, but for one week of the year she mates only with the most skillful to augment her powers. If aligned mating were to occur, her strength would be increased. However, she does not mate on Earth, for her Ego stands in the way of true mating. Also, your brother wins every year, an you are his cosmic mate, not Lilleal.

"The ceremony requires virgins, of which Atlantis is in short supply. The virgins lack all comforts and develop fear and apprehension. Try to be like a cornered animal in your consciousness, for Lilleal must approve all participants, and you must be chosen," Tzadkiel told her seriously.

"But you said sex was sadistic here. I am a virgin who has other ideas about love and sensitivity. Why should I destroy the dreams of my childhood? There must be another way to fulfill my destiny," Zallah questioned in agitation.

"No, this is the way to your brother, who is the fulfillment of your childhood dreams. After you mate, the destiny potential is controlled by both of you; without mating, neither of you can achieve your maximum potential. Keep your fear and anger. It will confuse Lilleal as to your real essence. Do not fear your brother; he is the other half of your True Self, and mating with him will be more than your imagined dreams: it is the key to your heritage and future, and is an alignment of the Essence in which all men and gods can share. I will take you to the palace tomorrow.

"Remember: you must willingly choose your own path. I can direct you, but the steps toward the future must be yours. Meditate on your future, and relax under my protection. I have little form energy left, and must replenish my depleted supply. I will retire now, and leave you to yourself, for soon you will be alone no longer. Even I vibrate in anticipation of the energy this event will unleash. Your future is mine also. I have faith that the Prince and the Princess can free the Earth," Tzadkiel replied, and then retired in exhilarated exhaustion.

Zallah looked around at her Godfather's serene home, and knew he was a holy man. She would prepare as he instructed, for she was not tired, but brimming with unanswered questions and feelings. The Sun set and the Moon rose, casting new colors through the crystal ceiling. She walked around the room and noticed a small table laced with fruits and nuts. Behind the table, in a niche in the wall, stood different colored crystal prisms, fabricated on stands of gold and silver. When she touched one, they all vibrated in musical tones and compositions, which took the last tension out of her body.

She walked outside and inhaled the perfumes of the floral fragrances of jasmine and gardenia, draped in abundance over the backyard canals; direct branches of four great rivers of Atlantis. Nightingales blended in with the sonata coming from the prisms inside, and she thought how life had great rewards in this hidden colony. She was ready to greet the future as she reentered the house. On her way to her room, she passed a scroll in another niche in the wall. She held it in her hands, and traced the geometric designs embossed on the golden sheet. She did not remember seeing designs like this before, yet she instantly knew the meaning:

> "What he thinketh is his heart; so is he.
> What he reasons with his mind; so shall be.
> What he fashions by his own hands; will be,
> the Essence of evolved Earth, for all of we.

IX

Tzadkiel and Zallah travelled to the direct center of the city, where the Pillar of Power stood between the pyramid and the cube. He explained that the pyramid was the temple, but they would enter the cube, which was the palace. The giant prism atop the cube reflected great concentrations of light into the palace. The great hall had walls of pure gold accentuated by thousands of candles which produced more pulsating flashes of light. The hall overflowed with the dissonant music and hysterical laughter of people over stimulated by drugs and drink. Before she could assimilate all the visions pulsing in and out of the light flashes, Tzadkiel bade her enter a side chamber where the virgins were being assembled. Some had been sold into slavery to the Palace to pay taxes; some had been kidnapped from foreign lands; she was here voluntarily to find her destiny.

The High Priestess, Lilleal, appeared to interview the virgins. Zallah thought her beautiful of form, but overstated. Lilleal was naked and proud; her nipples were painted red and adorned with rubies, and diamonds were intwined into her pubic hair. She thrust her imprudent nipples into the vision of each applicant, and asked what they knew and thought of sex. She eliminated them if they showed no agitation from fear. She stood in front of Zallah. Zallah was filled with agitation: not of fear, but of anticipation of her destiny. She let Lilleal smile at her emotional state. "What do you think of sex?" Lilleal asked.

"I don't know of sex, but I wouldn't adorn my body as yours is. Why do you paint your nipples, and glory in your nakedness?" Zallah said.

"Our bodies are our seats of power, our temples of form, and must be worshipped appropriately. I adorn mine to show my love for it. Does my nakedness frighten you? Yes, I see it does. That is good."

"Yes, I am afraid. Please release me from this ceremony. I do not want to participate. Release me. You will not be pleased by my performance." Zallah at last spoke some truth.

"You will perform. You are perfect, full of fear and distrust of your physical form. Shame of nakedness is a common denominator amongst the virgins. Join the chosen. Now I will explain the Ceremony so all can prepare," she said, "and panic," she thought to herself.

"The high lords of Atlantis must demonstrate mastery of their bodies and their sexual prowess. They must show mastery of the strong over the weak, it is one of the standards of Atlantis. With their phalluses erect, their pillars of power will rend your virgin territory. He who remains hard and strong the longest; he who tears the most virgin flesh; he who spills the most virgin blood; he will be deemed master, and will be my anointed mate for the holy week. As the mysteries command, he will bring his phallus, anointed with virgin blood, to infuse me with power," Lilleal proclaimed as she watched the terror growing on the young faces. Lilleal had them taken to the baths, shaking and frightened.

Zallah walked the corridor to the baths and wondered where Tzadkiel had gone, when he appeared before her with a strong handsome man who, though overtly masculine, was drugged and drained of his energies.

"Lucien, my Prince, this is Zallah, and I ask that you choose her in the ceremony tonight. Her family owes me a great debt they refuse to pay, and I would repay them with her suffering.

I would have her mastered by the best; her pain would be my pleasure," Tzadkiel smoothly lied.

Lucien was flattered, but some of his mind functioned above the drugged levels. "But you have refused to participate in ceremonies for many years, and complained of our decadence and waste," he remarked. "What has prompted this change?"

"I cannot hide from Atlantis forever. It is my destiny as well. Hiding is as much an excess as I accused you of. I felt this ceremony was the way to restart and reassert my part in Atlantis' future. Choose Zallah, and I will be part of your Victory, and part of the future here again. Through her pain, will I be repaid be her family. Choose her, and you will win this evening, my Prince," Tzadkiel replied.

"Atlantis needs the powers of all its Magicians, even those who have been temporarily blinded by the Light. I will choose her for you, but she doesn't look at me with fear, Tzadkiel. That will not help me win the contest," Lucien said, as he turned his attention to Zallah.

"I promise you will win with Zallah. Have I ever falsely prophesied?" Tzadkiel asked, and smiled at the Prince's interest in Mariella.

"No, you have always been known for your sight, that is why none could tolerate your visions of destruction. Even Lilleal fears your sight. If you say I will win with her, so be it. What say you, Zallah? You don't seem to be in awe, or frightened of me." Lucien stared into her eyes.

"No, I cannot fear you, it is not in my nature. But I do greatly fear the ceremony, for Lilleal did not paint a pretty picture of this evening.

"Pretty is plain. It is not beautiful, but paltry, and we in Atlantis do not accept anything that is not of great beauty or power.

"Only extremes are appreciated here; the rest slides by as unnoticed, as plainness is of no consequence. Your plainness will let my beauty shine in comparison. Your fear will pleasure us, your masters, and your great pain is my way of winning. That I already have remorse for your pain is a strange reaction for me. But strange emotions are also a potent stimulation. What an unusual day this is becoming. Here is a cream which is a strong opiate. After your bath, spread it on your vagina. It will numb the pain. I can't understand what compels me to do this, but you must be a good actress, and pretend excruciating pain tonight in the ceremony. It is the only way to win, and I am the Prince. I must always win. Practice your panic. It must be intense and overstated. Can you do this?" Lucien pleaded.

"Yes, I will help you win tonight. You'll have a rupturing, riotous time. I might be plain, but I'm not simple. I thank you for the cream, and I promise to act duly horrified. But even in your excesses, I must confess you cannot horrify me. No one will know of your kindness. I will scream so loud, they will all know that Lucien, the Prince, is the most potent phallus here," Zallah answered, laughing to herself. She joined the other virgins at the baths in the slave quarters.

The Prince watched her disappear, and his tenderness passed with her exit. The emotion slid from him, as he had no memory of expressing what he had been trained to regard as a weak emotion.

The virgins were allowed to bathe together in the hot perfumed waters. The heat and their togetherness help to relax them. They were purposely soothed and pampered so that later, unguarded of their emotions, their agitations and fears would redouble as they were retrapped by the sadism of Atlantis. The baths were designed in marble and the walls in silver, with waters flowing in from all four of the rivers through ducts, filling basins, and overflowing into a reservoir at the core.

The virgins were taken from the baths and covered with long silk robes that increased their comfort, and protected their modesty. They began to relax and forget their anxieties. They were led as a group back to the main hall where the noise reached a crescendo as everyone noticed them, and made ribald comments.

People everywhere were in pairs and groups, copulating and moaning in ecstasy; bodies devouring bodies. The visions and odors of rampant sex started to raise anew the panic of the virgins.

Twelve men were brought forth, adorned with diamonds and gold. The girls cried in fright when they noticed all twelve were naked, bearing enormous erections: raised, and painted red.

The silk robes were ripped off of the virgins and the crowds screamed their approval; their nakedness embarrassing them as the drugged masses drooled in anticipation. The twelve men came toward the virgins, each pointing to the girl of his choice. The Prince pointed to Zallah, as agreed. She might not fear the Prince, but she succumbed to the panic that spread through all twelve girls. Her fear was palpable, and the sweat poured from her pores, chilling her entire being.

The men returned to a raised platform in the center of the hall, a raised dais stood in the center where Lilleal reclined on a throne. The men sat cross legged on the floor in a circle around her, their red erections clearly visible and protruding.

Lilleal rose and went to the virgins. She took the first one and pushed her down on the phallus of the first contestant, which elicited a scream from the girl and cheers from the crowd. The odor of fear was potent, everyone chanting and yelling with each virgin's screams, as she was pushed onto the erection of a participant who then pulled her up and down upon his penis to increase her pain, thus proving his prowess.

Zallah was brought last to the Prince, and her scream was the loudest, as she was thrust upon him. The crowd echoed her scream as they shouted their approval. Zallah's scream was not an act, nor was it caused by physical pain, as the opiate prevented that. Her pain was born of outrage, as she was repulsed by the lust and sadism of the Atlantians. The people who many considered to be the height of the race, in reality were no more than snivelling, moaning, and lusting animals. Their heights were actually depths she had not imagined possible. But when she looked into the eyes of the Prince, all disgust left her, and she relaxed to the feelings of intense pleasure and belonging.

"To the man who stays hard the longest, rends the most virgin flesh, and is covered by the largest streams of red blood, goes victory; and me. For beauty is given only to the strongest beast," Lilleal chanted to the cheers of all.

Mariella felt the filling of her intrinsic emptiness with his presence. How an empty space existed within her. He showed her where, filling it and satiating her into subliminal supernal awareness.

Lucien moved her up and down, his shaft mesmerized by her vaginal lips, as he manipulated them lovingly. How ironic he thought, before this moment he complained that his world was limited to the confines of Earth, and now he glorified and centered on the true core of his worlds: the bud of her inner lips. He bent his head and kissed and suckled them. His future was now centered and circuited through his sister, as he pulled her up and down, and felt her stretching around him.

He was primeval life, pulsing in the seas of the Great Mother; warm and aware of the flow pulling him deeper towards a luminescence that fanned a deeper heat. Down through time, to the Essence of the beginning; the depths of eternity pulled into the center, as the desire to merge and join and give up the oneself to the whole self manifested in him. Then the one stream gushed and flowed into the fluidity of the other. The combinations of the two energy flows soared back out from the center through the cosmos; past comets, blazing in perfect complimentary spirals of electromagnetic balance. Lucien was always staggered by that first remembered, long awaited ecstasy that was cosmic mating.

The Prince and Zallah were not aware of the others. They were mated and whole, and their consciousnesses blended and soared through the cosmos. Instead of virgin's blood covering them, liquid gold ran down their loins.

Assured of the Prince's prowess, Lilleal was watching him in pleasure. But this turned to panic when she spied the golden liquid, and light pouring from them. She started to scream and pull her hair. "Release yourself from her Lucien," she cried. "Release yourself from your sister! You will ruin our destiny!" Lilleal tried to approach them, but was blocked by a huge surge of light which rose from them and spread through the building, passing through the crystals to the cosmos beyond. The Earth shook as the Light returned from above to shine upon them more intensely, and then branched to a shaft of Light which appeared before Lilleal. A figure appeared in the light that had more energy than form, and said, "You have failed Lilleal, and Luciel has lost his son again to the Light; for darkness is always relit by love. You cannot separate what has been reunited. The children are mated as they were destined to be. The whole cannot be severed now. All people must reawaken to the Light, for it is the only future," said Michael, his voice resonating through the hall.

"So, you have Lucien again, Michael, you and your simple daughter. But you will not have Atlantis or Earth. Take these two with you and go. We will succeed without him and your interference. You cannot change what we have created. Earth has succumbed to the darkness. Only the perfection of the strong will survive," Lilleal replied savagely.

"Darkness is absorption with no individual memory potential. That is not survival, but death. The children and I bring great pulses of Light, which provides definition and reflection for all who embrace it. There is a spark of light in the blackest darkness. It gives the promise of rebirth, and hope for all who open their eyes to see. The children will go from Atlantis, for she has reached her heights and now descends into death. This death is her destiny. Her rewards stem from you and Luciel and the natural outcome of Atlantis's self-inflicted wounds. Rebirth is ours, however. The Light is never defeated, only sometimes deflected. The three of us and other like beings of Light will realign the unbalances, and we urge all forms who sense this Light even minutely to leave Atlantis to the darkness she has embraced. The darkness that will engulf her," Michael preached, and he looked with tenderness at the children.

Zallah looked in awe at her Father. "Oh Michael, I have found you again, and I have found great pleasure with my brother. My future is as bright and grand as I was promised." Zallah and Lucien embraced Michael.

"Light is healing my wounds and redefining my existence. I feel centered again, and my destiny also is bright," Lucien affirmed.

"Yes, the future is auspicious for both of you together, as the Light of creation pours through you and Earth. Leave this place of unbalance and darkness, and tread the path of love for each other, and for all creation, which you are centered with," said Michael, and he smiled with love.

"Will you take us out of here, Father?" Zallah questioned.

"No, together you have the power to accomplish all. You must choose the paths of your destiny by yourselves. I have now returned my energy to Earth, and will facilitate and augment your choices. But the choices must originate from you and Lucien. Go to the sailboat Lucien has docked at the edge of the dark forest. Luciel helps his son provide for all circumstances, including his failure to prevent what he cannot prevent. You both have had all your powers returned to you. Lucien's powers are centered by your thoughts, as you are also centered by his in the ebb and flow of your heightened consciousness. The dark forest is no threat to you, for darkness is banished by your love. I will remain here a span longer to reawaken those who have ears to hear my message. The Light surrounds you, and you are now again a part of all of us in Light, as we are part of you. We will meet again in rebirth," Michael said, and he kissed them farewell.

"Let us travel the paths of destiny together, my brother. I am full of excitement for this new life, and I gladly seek actions. For the first time I can unleash my full imagination, though I admit there are things in your imagination that now, combined as ours, astounded me," Mariella said avidly, as she grabbed his hand.

Lucien too was inspired. "I am in awe of Life, and not just my own glorified part, for the first time in long ages. I seek fulfillment in shared love, which is a reversal of our polarity and the power potential of our joining. Our destiny awaits sister. Do you remember how much you love my ketch, Caprice? My father has her waiting at the coast; she's a perfect example of the balance of natural force and pressure, and we'll join there together most pleasurably and frequently. Together we will sail from the sunset of Atlantis to the sunrise of the rebirth of Earth. Our destiny awaits, as the future unfolds new frontiers."

X

Evelyn returned to awareness, and turned from the mirror to Tzadkiel. "Well, I admit you are my Godfather, and that was my past: the energy patterns have reconnected to my consciousness, and I know I have seen parts of my life cycle. But my brother my mate, and me a brood mare; this I wish to deny. If there is progress in evolution and free choice, then I wish to change the pattern and continue alone."

"Of course there is free choice. There is free choice as to what you achieve on Earth, and there is free choice as to what you perceive and achieve in Heaven. But you neglect the maximum and minimum potentials. To sever the cycle and develop your own Ego without relating to the whole is Luciel's wish, and there is far too much selfishness already on Earth. Luciel is so obsessed with Earth, that he has concentrated most of his energy here, resulting in Earth's greatest unbalance of negative energy. The whole is a combination of these polarities of energy in equal balance: negative and positive are both parts of the whole. Neither is complete or balanced without the other. Luciel's energy is a potent force. Aroused by anger and concentrated totally on Earth, they produce great negatives; thus the positive force necessary for balance must also be great. I came to Earth when you were young and not consciously connected to your Father. I took form to help protect your destiny on this planet. This I promised your Mother. I cannot release myself from this Earth form until you mate with your brother, and you cannot recircuit with your Mother, Marah, and your Father, Michael, until you mate with him. The Earth cannot rebalance to the whole unless your positive powers are united with your brother's equalizing negative energy. You have responsibility, as do all evolved beings, to the forward growth of creation; a return to the center of the two parts of the whole: positive and negative, in equal magnitudes. Then the center, in assimilation, evolves greater consciousness, which increases the positive and brings rebirth to the cycle. There is no good or evil in the cosmos; that is a value judgment of the unevolved. Negative energy is as integral to Life as is positive: form is as integral to evolution as is force, but it is only in the melding of the two parts that the whole is accomplished.

"You are regaining the energy patterns of your consciousness, but your powers are useless to Earth unless they are grounded with your brother. To deny your place on this path is to uncenter your self as Luciel has done, and as he has taught Lucien to do. There is already enough misdirected energy on Earth seeking Ego glorification: prideful people and governments who are vain and uncentered; religions that claim their visions are the only ones, when in reality they are only one part of the whole. Oneness exists only in the balance of polarity, not in its separation. The positive must mate with the negative, for only together are they whole.

"You are the daughter of Michael, and you must vibrate the positive and reach the center by joining with your equal negative. You cannot escape your inner nature: to do so would be to destroy, rather than to create. You cannot alter the Great Change that approaches. To achieve rebirth after death is to return to the roots, which at return always achieves a higher plane of evolution. Look now to your roots. I refuse to accept that you would deny my guidance and advice." Tzadkiel said with concern.

"No, Tzadkiel, I won't deny your guidance, but I'm not comfortable with it. I know you're trying to tell me that

Lucien is the hairy Prince in the other room; and to be honest, I'm revolted.

"See, you've found him. Fate is working. Now you must mate with him," Tzadkiel said, and he smiled again.

"Oh! my worst nightmare, a Prince of pricks who has little more to his personality than an erection. I'm to love him and to make love with him for the sake of my planet and evolution. This must be a colossal joke," Evelyn replied.

"Humor is a quality of gods as well as Man. Laughter is a positive energy force. When the two parts of the whole reincarnate separately out of the whole, they see their differences and would alter opposite polarity to fit their own image. But when their image is united to its opposite, they return as one to the center. They then realize what they had assumed to be opposite was merely other facets of itself, and they encompass those facets, and more. In the center is the sum of its consciousness, and also the sum of all other divergent, remelded parts of the whole.

"This realization is so staggering and fulfilling that the parts in the center have no desire to leave the oneness; they forget the struggle they underwent in the protection of the Self, which pales when one achieves the Overself.

"Then the Ancient One laughs, for the cycle was recircuited and he is glad. He knows the joke is that his laugh, which adds positive energy, rebirths the whole cycle, and all the parts must separate again to rebalance this positive thrust. Separating each time on a progressively higher plane, the parts fight to diverge, but they never achieve the growth they pursue until they seek it back in the center; reunited with opposite forces.

"In reuniting is such pleasure and awareness, they never wish to separate again. The gods would be gods and the men would be men, but the paradox is that each must be both. To achieve consciousness of the gods is to reach the center. To incarnate as Man is to travel to edges of the spiral. It is through the expenditure of energy from the center to the circumference of the spiral, and its return to the center, that the spiral moves forward. The irony is that Man wishes to deny the forces of the center, and the gods would deny the forms of the circumference: but they are parts of the same whole. The Ancient One laughs at both parts for thinking they could maintain separation or sublime oneness indefinitely, for all parts must continue to grow. There is neither separation nor supernal oneness until you see they are the same."

"All right Godfather, the joke is on me. I always find my brother in seedy places surrounded by beings claiming to be superior, when they are indeed very primitive," Evelyn replied.

"Good Mariella! Your sense of humor is returning, and you are thinking clearly. There is no superior or inferior, just stages from primitive to advanced. Lucien surrounds himself with primitives because only they are malleable, and believe in the concept of superiority. Also, Luciel has taught his son to think of human form as inferior to his pedigree, so he never lets him incarnate as less than a Prince.

"It galls Luciel that the Ancient One gave a son to Earth in his own image, and that humans are the denser forms of Star Children. He has Lucien reincarnate always as Lucien, always missing the point of diversity of form to increase his experience: for it isn't the form itself that designates a Prince; rather, it's in its return link to the energy that created it. Your brother is the Prince when he mates with you, as you then are his Princess.

"Together you can realign the unbalances of Earth and spread the Light for rebirth. Your importance is not to be a breed mare of forms, though you will produce aligned children of the new root race. But rather, your roll is as a producer of Light: energy released by your love and mating. That energy source is capable of creating many more balanced forms than your Earth body is capable of," Tzadkiel explained to her.

"Well, he thinks himself the stud stallion. I have seen his

arrogance, an he reeks of the false superiority you explained: he's unbalanced," she replied.

"Yes, your understanding and knowledge will unite with his aggression and experience to form your whole, and achieve balance. Without balance, life is momentary, not eternal. Eternity is a dynamic movement from center to circumference to center again, always balancing and always continuing with different speeds, reacting and interacting to send the spiral forward.

"The Sixth Race of Man is to begin. When the floods, volcanoes, and earthquakes occur more frequently, they foretell of the Great Change which precedes the rebirth of Earth. Man shall lose the technology he depends on, and once again return to his roots. This includes dependence on nature, the nature he thought his civilizations had tamed. When science and machinery are no longer available to him, he must go back to relying on nature and his planet Earth for sustenance and the meaning of Life. The same Earth he tried to conquer in his arrogance, he must respect and be in awe of again. To travel the oceans without fuel; to survive the poles of the planet without modern heating; to grow food without seeds; to amuse himself without television or radios; all requires recircuiting of the energy to the whole. Knowledge lost can only be regained by rejoining one's consciousness to the energy of the center. These patterns can be tapped directly from Earth's energy patterns, or tapped from ones own mind.

"Man will be in awe and fear of life once again because of his former structure: that which he felt was reality will be gone. What remains of Earth's patterns he must then readapt to. This tests his development and evolution, for only forms capable of adapting to the changed environment will survive.

"You and Lucien will show the glory of form in its reconnection to force, and how to receive the energy through this new and direct channel. You and Lucien will demonstrate the mating of force to form, so that form learns to receive its inspiration from force, and not from the adulation of its own form.

"The Sixth Race of Man, as all races before him, must rise from the material world once again, and reconnect to the spiritual worlds. Through love and sublimation Man can rebalance with the energy that not only sustains him, but also gives him purpose. One must tap into the power of the center, for only there resides the power of many.

"Returned to the animal world, civilized man loses his direction, as his Ego loses self-importance, for in the roots of the natural world he can sense his separateness and simplicity. But the key to his survival lies in his aligning with the forces of the whole; by returning the Light and love to the world from where he receives it, and by loving all the separate parts of Earth's whole: all his brothers, all animals, all life forms. Then he will have the awareness that they are his whole also. When populations are reduced to root races, the powers of Light can surround the darkness and mate with it to reinfuse its Essence. When people are few, the Angels are many.

"When you and Lucien mate, you show that the roots of the Animal Kingdom are in the Angelic choir. Together, you must love all forms on Earth. This connects them to the Light energy, which balances them. Then, all parts of Earth forces and forms can feel the pulse of the patterns of their planet, and march to the rhythm of the evolution of universe," Tzadkiel sermonized.

"That is an enormous responsibility, the reality you would have me accept and serve. These lessons seem above my grasp," she admitted.

"What you learn on Earth is what you have consciously chosen as your destiny; chosen when you were not incarnated as an Earthling. When you are out of form on Earth, you have the awareness and potential of the whole, but what you can assimilate of the whole is dependent on your development and knowledge: they are parts of enlightened imagination. What you choose to achieve on Earth is not only possible, but is also necessary to accomplish.

"What we conceive of, we create on all levels. We are responsible for all of our creations, and must judge these creations by ourselves before we present them for all in the center to review. What you think the whole to be, and what you say it shall be, is the whole you will assimilate. To lose faith in one's own creations is to sever the energy connections of your patterns, and negate your evolution's maximum potential. Where ever you are, on whatever planes of existence, what you imagine and say is what you create and give life to. Whatever visions of Earth you can align with, are the parts of Earth you receive. Whatever visions of Heaven you can align with, are the parts of the whole you will perceive. Nothing your mind can imagine is above your grasp, for the energy of mind is the energy of creation.

"Combine the potential of your imagination with the potential of Lucien's imagination, and you can understand how the power of creation grows, and evolution spirals forward.

"I must teach you to recircuit the patterns of your imagination and to open your consciousness to the powers of your mind development. It is time to look into the mirror again. Concentrate and look again into it. To understand what you have chosen to accomplish on Earth, you must look into the mirror of your Inner Self. Travel there with me," said Tzadkiel and his voice turned to the energy of speed. "Travel on the energy paths of your mind."

XI

Evelyn and Tzadkiel arrived at a river, calm and peaceful, whose sparkling waters streamed with swans, storks, egrets, and other majestic birds she could not name.

"Where are we Tzadkiel? This isn't a vision I'm watching. I'm here and I have awareness."

"Yes, we used the mirror a different way. We travelled great distances through our minds. This is where you come after Earth incarnations. It is your learning university: your present growth commune. Look at yourself," Tzadkiel said, as he pointed to her body.

Evelyn saw her skin was incandescent, with all of the colors of the prism pulsing through her aura. She had long red hair, with the tips of the nails on her toes and fingers bearing the impression of two twined crescent moons with a six-pointed star of gold above, and a silver five-pointed star below. "How is this possible? I am still Evelyn in my mind, but this is not her body."

"This is the body you have here, the body of Mariella. It is made of mind energy and is purer than your physical form. But as you are still in form development, your mental body takes this shape. As you evolve, you will attain more energy than form as you advance planes," Tzadkiel explained.

"Where is my Earth body?" she asked.

"It is back on Earth, sitting in front of a mirror."

"You look the same on Earth as you do here. Why don't I?"

Tzadkiel sat down on the supple grass and began to explain. "What you see of me is the form I take in order to return to the physical world to protect and educate you. My real shape, and those of my birth commune, are more gaseous than solid; but to facilitate our contact, I have the form you see. When a being has evolved beyond the worlds of form, past the worlds of mind, it becomes part of the world of spirit. As such, it is hard to put that concentration of energy into a small, solid state. What you see is a simple form in appearance, but full of complexities. When those of our worlds return to form, we do so to improve the whole by redirecting pure sources of Light into the density of the planes of form. We reinfuse ourselves, and evolve the denser energy of form into finer ones. As we return to elevate the planes of the slower forms, we elevate the whole, as well as our part of the whole.

"Remember: my birth commune and that of your Mother's is known as the 'Watchers'. We record and evaluate life energy on planes above the physical ones. Like the Ancient One, we journey to the physical worlds to take the Light from the center to the outer edges of the circumference of our life spiral. We give this Light as a forward thrust of energy, and we teach and demonstrate that the individual parts of the whole may hook up to the return, circulating power."

"Do you have the ability to take any form you wish?" she asked.

"On the levels past the physical ones, one learns to mold his energy into any shape or form. As you develop from form, the forms become secondary to the energy they house. That is Luciel's great unbalancing. He is past the worlds of form, but cannot free himself of his fascination and frustration with the physical worlds. He adds to this unbalance by concentrating his attention on Earth when Lucien is there, instead of pursuing his assignment: the testing and stimulation of all life forms of this level of evolution in many other galaxies. He is fanatic about Earth, because he sees it as an inferior evolution for

Lucien, and hopes the great unbalances he inspires men to build will blow Earth into the abyss, thus freeing Lucien from incarnating here. Luciel cannot otherwise break what your Mother had decreed. He ridicules Man so that Lucien will also think them inferior. He, and other beings like him, have even come to Earth in drunken orgies and taken the forms of animals to stimulate their matings with Earth women. Ridicule of form by force is an extreme double negative. We of Light return to Earth to give knowledge to form; to facilitate their recircuiting.

"Luciel is as tied to form as any force can be while still maintaining its energy speeds. This overindulgence in the physical causes energy unbalances within his own energy patterns that burn him and overflow to Earth. He is so close to the edge of the circumference, that he might hurl himself into the abyss instead of the Earth which he seeks to push there." Tzadkiel's speech reopened her awareness.

"I do remember. I am Mariella here, and I seek knowledge to grow, and to share that growth. I incarnate as different forms to increase the potential of my consciousness. This is my spiritual university, and Earth is where I take form education."

"Yes Mariella, this is your university; your growth commune. It exists as it was built: on a set of laws and paths that are its foundation. Its population is diverse in age and development, and many different courses of study are offered. Each individual studies to increase his knowledge and experience, and to return this understanding and energy to the whole commune to share. It is through complete development of the individual wherein lies its strength. To reach unity is a process of growth, experience, and learning: but first comes the development of the Oneself to make possible the knowledge and understanding of the whole self.

"Each college has its own shape, color, and themes of study, with the seven clusters of structures being situated in a circle. The center of the circle has a domed structure for the Grand

Master, surrounded by a large open air arena where all seven schools converge to review and share the lessons learned individually. Do you remember Lemuria? They were gentle giants in mind and spirit, and tried to pattern their Earth society after this university.

"You are a student of the Green School, and I am its Headmaster. We catalog and record all life forms of all evolutions. We in the Green School are also Watchers, for I bring the seeds of my birth commune here to continue evolution. We make mental images, or videos, of all life we encounter; then we share these videos with the entire university. We demonstrate the simplicity of form to produce the strongest power linkage, and we give additional light to all these energy patterns by surrounding them in love. As we take some energy from the forms to record them, we return the flow by giving them this extra energy of Light. By our love of all forms, even the densest, we spread positive energy throughout the cosmos," Tzadkiel explained.

"Yes, I remember now. I chose to study advanced polarity. Mating with the negative energy equal in magnitude to my positive was the goal of the lesson. Lucien is the counter balance to my energy. He is the negative that equals my positive."

"Yes," responded Tzadkiel. "The force expanded by the balancing recircuits both parts of the whole in order to advance their polarity potentials and conscious planes. That knowledge then advances all parts of the whole, which advances the planes of consciousness of the center."

"What university does Lucien belong to?" Mariella asked.

"Luciel has so fallen into form that he seeks only sensual stimulation: not lessons or knowledge, and he makes Lucien respond in his image. Out of Earth incarnation, Luciel and Lucien travel the Universe together, seeking to pleasure themselves and prove their superiority and right to rule over galaxies of life forms. They seek experience and action as does the Red School here, but they do not assimilate or share their experiences with any part of the whole. They both gallivant wildly and expend energy madly; what little they react with and absorb, they do not reconnect with the center, but share only with each other. Luciel is trying to prove the perfection of the individual before its return to the Essence. But to amass great surges of energy that are not harmoniously balanced with the Essence causes the individual to whirl at mad speeds to the edge of the spiral. The individual can then easily drop off the edge into the abyss, burned by the positive laugh of creation," Tzadkiel answered.

"As Evelyn would say, if they drop out too far, they'll drop off."

"That is right. Here you have all the possibilities and knowledge of Mariella, who is also Evelyn, and Zallah, and Sylph, and all the other forms you have been. So, now you know who your cosmic mate is," Tzadkiel smiled.

"Do you have a cosmic mate, Tzadkiel?"

"All beings and forms have mates. Higher energy forms have the potential for many mates, for they have the ability to read energy patterns and change their polarity to expend the equal energy required to balance both poles. We can mate with all types of form, for we know what vibrating speed of each polarity will align the union. The higher the development of the being, the more life it is capable of aligning in order to join the opposing forces that the whole can assimilate.

"But, 'as above, so below.' Love for all parts of the whole is the attribute of our Essence, and mating of the Overself moves Life. But the pleasure of mating with your spiritual partner, who is the exact balance of your full energy and the other half of yourself, gives the energy of Light most pure; it is the sum that totals the potential of your whole. Love for one's cosmic mate is more sweet and stirring than the polar love few men experience on Earth; when man's destiny permits awareness of his other self and provides him the opportunity to recircuit his energies to that union.

"My cosmic mate is also of the Watcher Commune: she is your Mother's aunt, Valerial. I will return to her when I complete this assignment at the University: when you graduate. Then you and Lucien will return with me to the plane of the Watchers. You will not graduate until you have completed your Earth polarity lessons with Lucien. Now, do you see the importance of your lesson? It is the lesson you planned yourself before leaving the school on your Earth field trip," Tzadkiel said as he looked at Mariella.

A voice from the knoll above the river interrupted them. "Tzadkiel and Mariella, how wonderful to find you! No one expected you back so soon! How excited the students will be! The center seminars on Earth experience are so stimulating, that all of us are eager for them. That's why this glade, a replica of the Garden of the Birth of Earth, is a popular place. All of us love the Earth creatures you have created here. I can watch these birds and animals for longer spans than I give to my studies. Oh, Tzadkiel, please don't tell Tzadek I said that," gushed a young girl in blue robes.

"Hello Dianah, and please slow down. We are not here to reassimilate. Mariella's Earth study is not yet completed. We came so Mariella can refocus the theme of the Earth thesis she is preparing. Mariella is still connected to Evelyn of Earth. Do you remember Dianah, Mariella?"

"Of course I know Dianah, she's a good friend. Where is Pelah?" Mariella asked the girl.

"Pelah is in incarnation on Beleron, and I await my next field trip to Ebony. Have you mated with Lucien yet? I have always wondered which was better: a mate like yours who is only available in reincarnation, or mine, only possible when out of form incarnation," Dianah pondered.

"Well, don't we share the experience of both in center council?" Mariella responded.

"Shared knowledge is one thing, and personal experience

is another. At least I'll get to choose either path after graduation. I miss Pelah, and my form lessons are not quite as motivated as yours. You can't wait until your field assignments, and I always wondered if that made you the better student; or was it Lucien that always motivated you to Earth?"

"I am a good student, and Earth lessons are more motivating to me than you imagine. I admit Lucien is part of my assignments, but not the motivation! Right, Tzadkiel?" Mariella stated emphatically.

"It was Mariella's motivation we were just discussing and regraphing. Are you ready to return to Earth?" Tzadkiel said, as he smiled at his goddaughter.

"Yes Godfather, I will return and complete my course as planned. I won't drop the theme on polarity. I can only hope my enthusiasm will increase for the lab work." Tzadkiel looked puzzled. "You know, the phallic probes," she replied, and he laughed.

"Goodbye Dianah, we return now to Earth. Mariella is impatient to prove the polarity power potential," said Tzadkiel smiling. "Mariella is becoming a Master of Earth's seed sciences."

XII

Evelyn and Tzadkiel returned to their physical bodies, still seated in front of the mirror.

"Godfather, I realize that my super consciousness would sacrifice my strong Ego by mating with my brother, allowing us to achieve forward progress on the path of evolution and expand both our consciousnesses. But back in my physical being, I am still repulsed by him," Evelyn admitted.

"Not repulsed, Mariella, just in opposition. That is the lesson of polarity. You are both halves of one whole; you are a Watcher, and he is a Mover. His aggression must be balanced by your knowledge and understanding, so that his motions meld, not manipulate. Separated on the physical plane, you are polarity opposites, and your energy of polarities here would repel each other. But you must transform the energy from repulsion to recircuiting.

"The Earth is near the fluxes of the Great Change: the death of the old, and rebirth of the new. You must implant the energy patterns all around you into your memory, for that memory, balanced by his momentum, will enhance your cycle of Earth Studies. Then you can return to your growth university with a completed course to share with the Grand Master, the Circle Council, and all of the other students.

"Look always to the Light, for therein lies your understanding of the past, and your beacon for the future. Your powers are returning to you; use them in balance. Go mate with

Lucien, that your father may return to you, and I can leave the density of the Earth and await you at the Green School. I know you will fulfill your responsibility to your family, if evolution itself isn't enough of a motivation. Go Mariella, and accomplish your destiny. As your Headmaster, I will judge your path; but as your Godfather who loves you, I want happiness for you as well as advanced degrees. I trust you will do what is right for you, and on a personal level I'll always support your choices. But as your Headmaster, I must admit that if you make choices that disregard your education, you risk failure, and must repeat the course until deemed passable. But this is unnecessary advice for one of my best students. Farewell, Mariella," he said as he gathered her in his embrace.

Evelyn soundly kissed him. "Do not worry Tzadkiel. How could the best Headmaster have anything but the best students? How could the most caring Godfather produce callousness in the child? I go to Lucien that I may mate with him and release you from your Earth form. Maintaining this form for me when I'm sure your energy is used to more rarefied planes is a sacrifice of love. I thank you for your education, and the teachings that enable me to see my path and seek it. Farewell Tzadkiel. I know you'll love my thesis."

Evelyn reentered the main room. People were copulating in varied groupings around the Prince. A young girl was standing in front of a sofa with her arms supporting her on it, bent over as the Prince mounted her from behind, biting her neck as he pumped and panted in passion.

Evelyn was disgusted and looked for Laurel. Laurel was in a foursome with a penis balanced above her in her mouth, and one in her behind, while the girl below her sucked her cunt. Evelyn made eye contact with Laurel, and Laurel jumped up at the look of disgust on Evelyn's face. The rest of her foursome went sprawling. "Why are you looking so disgusted, Evelyn? In all the years you've watched me fuck, I've never seen that look before."

"Sorry Laurel, the look wasn't for you. You're my friend, and I always see you in a good light; even with cocks in all of your corners. The look is for the Prince. God, he's awful; so animalistic. You're lucky he didn't choose you. He's one overproud prick who's into subduing, not giving pleasure," Evelyn pouted.

"Some women like to be subdued physically. He could fuck me anytime, and I assure you it would be pleasure: extreme pleasure. I realized tonight though, he doesn't choose women our age. We're left for group seeding. He only chooses young and beautiful girls for himself. What a shame. I'd let him put his overproud prick, as you call it, through any pore of my body," Laurel joked.

"You might see his value, but he leaves me cold. But I can't let my family down. I must mate with the Prince. Do you think I make a mystic martyr?"

"Mate with the Prince? Mystic martyrdom? Let your family down? Where have you been? Have they drugged you?" Laurel asked in concern for the mental state of her friend, who normally was Laurel's balance. Even in the most absurd situations, Evelyn remained calm, and never gave in to the physical satiations Laurel reveled in.

"You've always told me that my watching without participating would catch up with me. It has. I'm not giving in to my physical nature, but I must stop ignoring it. I've realized that to ground my spirituality, I've got to Earth it in sex," Evelyn responded.

"You're going to release the spiritual side of your nature by fucking? You always said that fucking was wasting energy without love to transcend it, and that you didn't need love; so, you had no use for fucking strangers when your own fingers were more capable of providing orgasm than a probing prick. Now you are telling me that sex is the answer to your spiritual quest. Wake up, Evelyn. They sure gave you the hard sell. You must be on drugs."

"Relax, Laurel, I'm not on drugs. But I have changed planes in my consciousness. The properly aligned pleasures of the physical union are delights on all levels, even those above form. Sex is a motivating force on all levels. What we can understand by correlation on Earth, we can apply to correlation in the heavens. Even Archangels fuck, believe me, but they call it fusing. The Prince's prick is my power hookup. I'm not seeking pleasure from him: rather, the power his penis can channel into me."

"Evelyn, I think it's time we leave. You've watched over me many times, and now I must return the favor. You're delirious. Come, I'll take you home," Laurel said as she gathered Evelyn into her arms.

"Thank you my friend, but I'm not out of my mind; I'm in it for the first time in years. Don't take me home. Take me over to the Prince. I need help with the first few steps, that I may face the future."

"Calm down, Evelyn. I've never seen you so agitated. Where is that famous cool you demonstrate in court and in all the courses of sexuality I've taken you to?" Evelyn smiled, and Laurel gave in. "All right, I'll take you over to the Prince, but I'll not watch you make a fool of yourself. I'm leaving. My sexual satiation is complete tonight, and I couldn't watch the ice princess melt." Laurel took Evelyn over to the Prince and said, "Prince, this is my friend Evelyn." Then Laurel turned from them, and left the apartment."

The Prince looked over Evelyn as he rated her physical appearance. "You don't have the beauty necessary to be a seed mother, and I've already given my performance this evening. You're welcome to come again. I know how Earth women look forward to the potent pleasures only I can show them, and the seeds of the new world only I can give them," Lucien replied as he dismissed Evelyn.

"Thank you for the honor Prince, but I don't see myself as a brood mare, and from the bruises you disperse, I find it hard to believe you give pleasure when all I see is pain in your physical force. It is hard for me to equate ruptures with rapture." Evelyn retorted.

"Pain and pleasure are both sides of supremely developed physical powers. Fucking with me is a physical art, as well as a physical act," Lucien replied defensively.

"I'm sure you're the best prick in the physical world, but I am a Watcher, with a message for your Father, Luciel."

"You are a Watcher, part of the commune of my Mother? Ha, mental creatures who have no participation in matter for fear it will unbalance them. You could never relax your body to give or receive pleasure with it. I bet my prick makes you nervous," said Lucien, and he shoved his in front of her face.

"Splendid physical specimen, but not my type or fear. Didn't you hear me? I have a message for Luciel."

"Luciel told me to avoid all Watchers, for they try to belittle our importance in evolution," stated Lucien.

"Belittle you! How could we tarnish the natural brilliance you emit? No, I have great respect for your Father's powers. He controls the pressure build up of the Polar Changes. Has he not discussed this with you?" Evelyn questioned.

"Of course he discusses the future with me. It is my future that is his greatest concern, and he has sacrificed much to insure a future worthy of my heritage. What information do you have that would interest him?" Lucien inquired.

"Would the location of your sister on Earth be considered important?" Evelyn replied sarcastically

"My sister! Yes, my Father and I are concerned about her vengeful nature. She always tries to abort our carefully devised plans for Earth. She tries to sever the Earth connections we put great effort in developing. She is a Watcher also. Why would you betray her whereabouts?"

"There is no betrayal on the paths of Evolution. The end justifies the means. Does not Luciel stress this? I believe for all concerned that this evolution of Earth must be different. I have a responsibility to this change: one that overrides my allegiance to the Watchers. I have this information, but I will only give it to Luciel personally. Do you think he will be pleased if you don't arrange this meeting?"

"I don't understand my Father's passionate concern for my sister. She has no great powers, and I can't sense her, so she has no importance to me. One moment he agrees with me that she is of no consequence, and the next he rages at her potential to destroy our plans and ruin our creations. I don't care about her, but it is true he cares too much. Thoughts of discovering her whereabouts on Earth unbalance his perfection. Yes, he will wish to know your information. Maybe this will release him. All right, I will take you to him. Meet me at the train depot at nine tonight," promised Lucien as he turned to leave.

"The train station? Is Luciel on Earth?" Evelyn asked.

"No, my Father is on the seventh moon of Vesperion," Lucien replied.

"So why don't we go into the other room and focus through the mirror that we may mind travel there?" Evelyn suggested.

"Luciel has trained me never to leave my physical form. I would never leave my body unprotected, for other forces could harm it, and even sever its connection to the rest of my self. My physical form is an achievement of perfection, and I would never jeopardize it. We will travel on my space flyer. My Father never leaves me on Earth without appropriate transportation. Transportation helps facilitate my rule of Earth during the Great Change, and enables me to visit him. Luciel rarely comes to Earth, though he rarely stops thinking of it. Meet me later at the train station, and I will take you to Vesperion."

XIII

Evelyn stood in front of the train station and waited. A red sports car with Lucien in the driver's seat, pulled next to the curb. She approached the car, and he opened the door.

"Why did you have me meet you here if we are driving?" she asked.

"I had to make sure you were alone. I've been following you since you left the apartment. You've made no contact with anyone. I have to be careful. There are too many trying to thwart the plans Luciel has made for Earth's future," Lucien replied.

"I have contacted no one. But you forget: a Watcher can make contact by mind powers, and needs no instrument of form to assist communication. You have nothing to fear from me. I told no one of this meeting."

"I do not fear Watchers or any other force. I control forms and rule them. I am always uneasy, however, when dealing with thoughts of my sister. She alone has the power to alter my evolution, and she derives this power by sapping mine. I lose Luciel's respect when I lose my zeal for pressure building on Earth. My sister traps my force in her form, and only in avoiding that trap will I make my Father proud." They continued to drive out of the city until they pulled up to a deserted farm. "Here is my space flyer," Lucien said gleefully.

They left the car and entered the barn, wherein stood a long cylindrical ship which they boarded. The inside of the space flyer was as luxurious as his car, with padded leather seats and furs for carpeting. One half of the ship was filled with panels of glowing instruments, and the other half with a lounge equipped with a thick, elliptical viewing window. They took off. The sense of speed was no greater than the sports car, though they passed from Earth and her solar system, and continued beyond, as stars twinkled through the window.

"This is amazing, and so advanced of Earth transportation. No wonder you must hide it. What NASA would give to see this," Evelyn gasped.

"I told you I take physical transportation very seriously. Man will not achieve efficient space travel until he changes his concept of fuel. Even Atlantis had better space flyers than modern Man. Higher beings gave Man the power of light through crystals. He flew high, until through his inferiority to control various powers which he released, he blew up his world. Knowledge given to those who cannot use it is the fallacy and weakness of evolution. Man has abused gifts that other beings have given him, and has no sense of the evolution of progress he wastes. Luciel and I would conserve this waste of power, and let Man blow himself into oblivion, as is his own inclination," Lucien explained.

"Aren't you afraid that to lead men into oblivion takes you to the edge of yourself?" Evelyn replied.

"The edge is what my father and I were created for. New realms are only possible by exploration, and in all exploration, only the strong survive."

"Exploration is fundamental in evolution, but that knowledge the strong must give back to the weak so that all may survive; the positive force is grounded in forms, lest it fall into a state of energy fragmentation that passes over the edge," Evelyn countered.

"It is energy wasted on the weak that slows evolution. The future is deserved only by those who wield energy and eagerly participate in the expansion of evolution in the physical worlds.

Watchers don't participate: they observe, and can't even deal with the reality they observe, for they are afraid to partake of the pleasures of the physical world. After all, this was the purpose of creation: to explore the pleasures of the physical world by taking form and experiencing them."

"But physical awareness must develop to spiritual awareness such that the pleasures you covet are shared by all the worlds. The spiritual created the physical so that the physical would evolve awareness of itself and of its origins. This combined plane must be recircuited for the creation to create, and return the energy to the center where it was born." Evelyn argued.

"Watchers are always debating the purpose of evolution, but that is passive energy. Beings like yourself can recite the pleasures of physical form, but you can't experience them. I'm sure you're a prude on every level of your being. Why bother to come to Earth if you can't experience the pleasures of Earth form? You have the power of mind travel; why remain here?" Lucien retorted.

"Earth is my field assignment; an assignment of body and mind. It is my responsibility to record its life forms and energy. Owing to this, I am not insulated from their pleasures or pains. I do not seek self-gratification and glory as you do, and so my pleasures are greater, as they originate in thousands of forms beside myself outside myself, brought through myself. I know it is hard for you to conceive of pleasures that are not centered in your prick," Evelyn countered.

"Ha! You're angered into a personal attack on me. Congratulations, I didn't think you had it in you. However, we have a distance further to travel, and I'm bored with your philosophy. Don't push the boredom to anger. If you can't change the subject, I'll enter alpha state and avoid you," Lucien smiled.

"Tell me what you know of your Mother," Evelyn said to change the topic.

"From politics to the personal. You're trying to do a Watcher profile on me: analyzing my personality. You're manipulating me, and pushing my anger," Lucien seethed.

"Well, you are a pusher; you admitted you admire pushing boundaries and rules of evolution. Why criticize me for imitating you?" Evelyn countered.

"That's good. One round to the Watcher who has manipulated my anger into amusement. Pushing it will do you good; maybe you can make other changes in yourself. Believe me, you don't know what pleasures you've been missing on Earth. Looking at you, I'd say you miss pleasure everywhere; but Earth has some special delights: lots of comely cunts."

"I won't be baited by your words, for I too love Earth. It's full of wondrous beauty, and is teeming with Life. You might be able to stimulate some life forms with your prick, but it can't compare to what I can assimilate of Life through my consciousness, which is not centered in my cunt. You must have great conflicts with your Mother," Evelyn countered.

"Back to my Mother again. I have no visions or memories of her, but I have animosity for her. She rejected my Father. She did not reciprocate his passion, which remains as intense today as it originally was, and is his only blindness. She has not appeared in our lives; yet she has not disappeared, for his pulsing passion for her is never appeased: thus, it festers on. Thoughts of my Mother are the chains on his freedom, and the frustration to our plans. I do not think of her; he does enough of that for us both. As far as I'm concerned, she is that part of my past that is best forgotten, as is the sister she created to consume me. He is weak when he agonizes over her loss, and weakness suits her purpose, not his. I have no future in the rest of my family," Lucien responded with savage bitterness.

"Strange, I can't picture Luciel mourning a lost love."

"My Father seeks perfection to gain her respect, but she punishes him by embracing the weak and helpless, giving them the love she denies him. Love is a vast waste of energy. It has confused and consumed my Father. I'll have none of it. There are mates a-plenty throughout the galaxies, without making the commitment of love. If I break my pattern from my sister, I will break my Mother's hold on me. That, I hope, will also release my Father. Then he will be free of his obsession, and I will free my destiny so that the two of us together might explore new boundaries and expand our perfection."

"Perfection is not expanding, it is restricting. It is a value judgment which will limit you to the worlds of form. Reliance on that false idea will constrict you, not free you. You will limit the new realms of growth and experience by sacrificing yourself to that principle. Death is a necessary potential for rebirth, but it is not its purpose. Your pride and your prick waste your potential; they don't increase it."

"Your conversation wastes my potential and angers me. We will soon arrive at Vesperion, and I would not have Luciel see my anger. Amuse yourself. I go to alpha state," Lucien retorted.

"What do you imagine in alpha that calms you?"

"I don't go into alpha state to calm myself, for I am not balanced in inactivity, but in motion. I concentrate on pleasures that excite me and revitalize my purpose. I love the best part of new colonization: when I use all my sensory powers on the primitive women, they adore me. My seed is needed to improve the flow of science and technology, and for pure adventure; for I use my most potent tool in the name of genetics. I remember especially the planet Silka. There we all appreciate pleasures shared, and the women worship my prick. There, life forms live in the warm, gushing liquids of its oceans; and in sex, all parts of me, not just my rod, are in its watery womb."

Evelyn watched him enter alpha state, and noticed his erection. She realized he would not try to mate with her, and that this time she had to change polarity. She had to be the aggressor. She had learned the lessons of the past. Before he could react, she opened his pants and sat herself on his erection.

They both moaned at the unexpected ecstasy. Desire rose in her like a tidal wave as her arms entwined him. She felt his lips upon hers, and her body opened more over his. Her skin sang, and her body's juices rushed, flowing to a climax as he continued kissing her.

She drew away from him, panting as an animal in a mating ritual, and dropped her clothes. He dropped his clothes also, noting how time seemed to move slowly when they were apart, and how, when he mounted her again, that suddenly time sped up.

They groaned together, and took each other in frenzy and heat; hands scratching, lips nipping. Quickly the second wave of pleasure peaked and ebbed. Then they slowed the pace and caressed each other in glory. She touched him everywhere, and noted that the hair on his head and chest was silky, while that on his penis was strong and springy.

He kissed where he had bitten, and his tongue reached everywhere his hands and teeth had not. They moved in unison as one being, and after another climax, lay holding each other, as if the whole world lay between them. As he soothed her flesh, his mind opened and he knew he had always loved his sister.

"Is this what you mean by great pleasure, my brother?" Mariella teased.

"Yes, my sister. This is pleasure I can't deny or explain. Pleasure so intense, it borders pain," Lucien smiled.

"Pleasure balancing pain: a part of the lessons of polarity. The Light will not burn you, Lucien. Release yourself from your body, that we can achieve the higher planes of pleasure again. Cosmic mating is awesome!" Mariella purred.

"What a sense of speed I feel," Lucien answered as he started caressing her sensually and seriously.

"My form controls the speed, Lucien. Give in to it. Release yourself to the Light," Mariella whispered in passion, as he pummeled anew.

XIV

Lucien and Mariella returned to their physical bodies as the space flyer landed on the desert moon of Vesperion.

"Oh Lucien, I love you. You are a part of me, and together we are more, much more than I thought I or we could be," Mariella said in wonder.

"Yes my sister, I am back in alignment; full of love for you, as if my consciousness awakened from a coma. I can't understand why my Father tries to prevent our mating, for it gives me balance and direction. Through your eyes I can see my blindness," Lucien answered, as he embraced her.

"Talk about blindness: the light and heat here are overpowering. Why does your Father live in a desert?"

"The desert is a prime example of survival of the fittest. Here, the weak die; only the strong and clever live: his kind of place," Lucien replied.

"I'm not sure I'm ready to meet Luciel. His feelings are so intense toward me, and when he discovers we are mated, he'll hate me more." Mariella was frightened.

"Do not fear my Father. His feelings are always intense. Be glad I inherited his passionate nature." he laughed. "Mariella, we are joined. We are a whole. Luciel will accept us together or alienate us both, and he would never alienate me. Come, let us go to the palace and diffuse your agitation in the security of my strength." Lucien led her to the palace, a replica of Versailles as ornate, elaborate, and lush as the desert oasis it stood upon.

Inside the grand hall sat Luciel, surrounded by golden mirrors, statues, and paintings from Earth. The most beautiful art, and the Archangel most beautiful of form, were perfect reflections of the potential of physical grandeur.

Michael appeared before Luciel. They were in contrast with each other: one light and energy, the other dark and form-bound. "Michael, what a pleasant surprise. It has been eons since you've visited me. Have you come to see the Earth art collection I've assembled? The most complete example of the best of the worst," joked Luciel.

"No, Luciel. I'll be interested in your collection when you donate it to the university. No, I'm here to greet the best example of your worst nightmares. The children have arrived. It's time for a family get together." Michael said, and he laughed.

"Family get together? You'll be disappointed, Michael. Lucien is coming, but he has avoided your daughter and your desires to join them. He had discovered how to break the pattern." Luciel taunted.

"They come together, and they are already mated. The pattern is continued, and you cannot destroy Marah's concept of her creations, nor change her will of their potential," Michael retorted.

"Lucien had been trained to avoid beings like your daughter and you. He despises what you think and detests the forms you adopt."

"You can confuse his mind, but you can't sever his instincts. As has been decreed and destined, the children have rejoined what you have separated. This you can never prevent," Michael affirmed.

"Well, maybe I should approach this in a new way. This time I will encourage both of them to see the reality of the imperfections of human evolution. The children are entitled to more powers in the galaxies. Being tied to this feeble group of creatures and this paltry planet retards the potential of their progress to the full potency of the powers they have inherited," Luciel mused.

"Planet Earth is their heritage, and they must grow with it. They must learn the rules of creation and evolution there before they have other worlds to guide. The powers they inherited are of the Earth; they only receive the potential when they are grounded on that planet. Have you forgotten the essence of eternity? Are the vast reaches of time now beyond your grasp that you would seek to slow seconds? You have lost your centering through your physical obsessions and overindulgence, and in the paradox of your fanaticism to see other beings grounded and the physical Earth destroyed."

"Physical specimens without beauty or strength were not meant to survive. They demean the perfection of evolved forms, for only perfect individuals should continue in creation," Luciel countered.

"Survival is a necessary test of evolution, and your task to perform. We have never denied this, but you have lost the whole in concentration on its parts. You see only individual parts and not the whole. These parts are so amplified in your vision that you would discard all parts except those of your choice for the potential of the whole. But you have forgotten that the whole is the sum potential of all its parts, and that in the simplest part is the potential for the strongest connection to the center. In Light is the reflection and definition of all colors, but in darkness there is only absorption with no individual memory intact. What you glorify to achieve becomes meaningless," Michael reminded Luciel.

"But that is the essence of creation, to take the wasted and unevolved energy and remold it into the strong and powerful," said Luciel with misguided conviction.

"Luciel, your impatience and rigidity are the cause of much imbalance and misdirection on Earth and other galaxies where beings like yourself try to spread their own self importance. The importance of the self is in its sacrifice for the whole, which includes all its parts and none to the exclusion of the others. We of the whole would exclude no one and nothing; even you are a part of our whole and we await your returning to us. I will not tolerate your desire to destroy the destiny potential of my daughter and your son, for Earth is where that potential must grow. Our children will be Prince and Princess together of an Enlightened Earth. I will not let you alter that course."

"Then prepare to fight again. I will continue to try to break this pattern. That is my right and my own creation," Luciel replied.

"Creation involves fulfilling a complete cycle, not in glorifying small parts of it. Remember, novas burn brightly for moments only to die in the abyss, but comets travel at slower speeds, maintaining connection to the center and their own identity through eons," Michael explained.

All evolution has its risks. Adapt or Die. Weed out the mutants and weaklings. Only allow the superior races and creations to survive and continue; that is the goal of growth."

"Have you lost connection to all your knowledge and education? Superior and inferior are value judgments of the physical worlds you would glorify. These concepts do not exist on the planes above them. All elements have the potential of the whole even though they revolve around the center at different speeds. It is true; speeds increase as you approach the center, but the slower speeds of energy at the circumference are still permeated by the center and carry the same seeds of conscious creation. Every part has glory, beauty, power, and potential when united in the core. Nothing that seeks to sever the connections will achieve eternity. You stretch the limits of your potential, Luciel. Soon you must recircuit or die," Michael answered.

"I'm touched by your concern, but do not fear for me. I

will realign when I have completed my part and my potential. I was created to stretch the limits and boundaries of evolutions. That has been my assignment, and I am achieving what I was born to create. Remember, there is no death at any level, for death always triggers rebirth. That is a rule of evolution. If my essence is perfect, how can I be less? I can avoid death by always achieving rebirth."

"Your pride is astounding," replied Michael. "You, an example of constant rebirth? Ha! Your idea of perfection in power of form is death. Rebirth is only in the center, and in this center no part has more meaning than any other or more beauty than any other, as all are reflected together. When there is death of your selfishness and your misdirected pride, then shall you be reborn. Here come the children. Let us debate no more. This is a time for celebration, not discussions." Michael turned toward Lucien and Mariella.

Lucien embraced Luciel as Mariella hugged her Father. "We are here to celebrate the rejoining of our families and the future bright with promise for our children. May they inherit the maximum destiny they are entitled to. Right, Luciel?"

"Right, Michael, on this we do agree. We both want the maximum potential for our children." Luciel handed them all goblets of wine. "We are both glad to toast the future of them both, and it can be grander than you dare to suspect."

"I'm glad you're agreeable, Father, and that you accept Mariella as my love and mate. She is the delight of my physical form which amplifies the whole of my being. Due to your interference, I can only achieve this satisfaction in Earth incarnation. So don't start again to belittle Earth, which is its physical centering." Lucien raised his goblet. "To love shared. To our families rejoined."

"Love and Earth are a waste of time, Lucien. You know they retard the strength of the whole, and your whole is diminished by them both," Luciel seethed.

"The whole is never diminished by its parts," answered his

son, "but the parts can diminish their own potential when they alienate themselves. This whole creation of Earth and all its creatures and energy will balance in the Light together. We are committed to this; it is the natural creation of our love that extends love of all creations on Earth. Would you deny me the rewards of love and cosmic mating because you are denied this, Father?" Lucien questioned.

"Maybe, Lucien. Maybe my Ego envied yours, but I have always wanted the best for you and for you to be the best. I have concentrated great amounts of energy toward your development and future, trusting that in the progression of evolution toward perfection, the son would become stronger than the father, and I will glory in the day you push past me. Have your love and your Earth and grow. I wish that more than you, but do not forget that power and force drive creation, and that the strong, like you, my son, will expand creation. I might not have the mate of my choice, but I know the love of a father and his son." Luciel embraced his son. "Because of that love I find it hard to tolerate what is inferior on this Earth and will weaken your strength when you give your energy to it."

"Oh Father, you have missed the point of love, for in the Light nothing is inferior. The strong become stronger when they strengthen the weak for then they center the energy and move to a higher plane. Give and you receive. Evolution comes with sacrifice and sharing; only then do we attain growth and amplify creation by our reflection of the recircuiting of creation. Creation is loving, not ruling; laughing at the imperfection of ourselves, not ridiculing the different levels of each other," Lucien said passionately.

"Nonsense, higher beings were meant to rule, to set examples. Your eyes are clouded by lust for your sister. I understand all too well. She is her Mother's daughter. But this mating will weaken your purpose, so I hope the pleasures are great," Luciel admonished.

"Weaken me. No, the endless sex we seeded over endless

galaxies spent me. This mating with Mariella realigns me with the whole. Then I wield the power of the center, which is the sum potential of all powers combined. You are aggressive, selfish, and ruthless; and you relish in your right to rule. But it is you who are wasting energy. You are trying to become a super power so as to command Mother to love you. But you have forgotten that to consummate that love would return you to the center, and there you would be no greater than any other part and equal to all," Lucien smiled.

"Of course I know what cosmic mating is; I'm not a fool. But I will return to the center when I have achieved my individual perfection. Then Marah will be proud to mate with me," Luciel replied.

"Mother is proud of all life, Father. You're trying to prove an empty issue. Beware your perfect physical development doesn't evolve at the expense of your spirituality, for then your energy will not be capable of recharging, and will discharge into unbalanced surges that could burn even you. A God who becomes a man and prefers his physical form to the exclusion of the forces channeling it becomes the same as the man who does not direct his form to the energy for guidance. In the center, the god is a man and the man is a god," Lucien retorted.

"I am an Archangel, not a man. Never could I be a man, for humans are weak and self-destructive," Luciel replied.

"Man self-destructs in the imbalanced energy you offer him, but beware you don't destroy yourself also. You are the great tester, and I will always love you, but you will be accountable for not sharing the results of the testings with the whole that evolution improves in all its parts. You will see the imbalance your manipulations have caused. I still believe you are the strongest and most beautiful of the Archangels, but you too must experience cosmic mating to achieve your potential. You waste the real greatness you have and can achieve," Lucien smiled.

Mariella and Michael continued to embrace and kiss each other, smiling as they listened to Lucien and Luciel arguing.

"They do go on Mariella, your mate and his Father. I too wait for the day when Lucien is stronger than Luciel. Maybe then my brother will return to our commune. I too always argue with Luciel, but I love him also and fear his independence will widen his separation from our whole. I'm so thankful that we are always in accord," Michael said lovingly to his daughter.

"Yes my Father, we are always one, and I am thankful to share that again. I also love Lucien, and this conflict tears him apart. I wish I could do something. Should I try to mate with his Father that I may balance him?" Mariella asked.

"You are clever my daughter, but Luciel is too powerful for you to balance now. In the future, after all Earth Evolutions, which it is not for you to understand now, you will have evolved power to balance higher and more complicated energy. Then, someday, you will mate with me as well as Luciel, for that is the potential of growth of all our children. Now, though, your path is centered in your brother and on Earth. Balance the energy and be content, for this is your present maximum potential. Align this circuit and all of the center will celebrate with you. Remember, evolution is one controlled step at a time, for to attempt a giant leap forward you must be balanced or fall. Look at Luciel," Michael explained.

Mariella looked at her mate and his father and she realized both of them were of her whole and of her family. Her maximum potential was related to Lucien's, but Lucien's maximum potential was also related to Luciel's. There must be something she could do to balance.

"She was the daughter of Marah. Marah could balance Luciel. The cycle would not grow for her until it could grow wholly for Lucien. Lucien needed Luciel in his whole as she needed Michael. Mother could show Luciel what real power was and who was the stronger. Mother, she thought.

Mariella imagined a giant golden chalice overflowing with liquid moonbeams and stars and golden shafts of light. The vision pulsed out of her consciousness into form before them all. Marah sent her energy to enter the chalice, and then the energy poured out over the golden cup and through Michael, Mariella, and Lucien.

Luciel saw Marah and saw her energy entwine with the other three, and he was filled with longing and jealousy. "Don't exclude me Marah. Please don't exclude me again. I love you so, and I devote my life and energy to you in order to be worthy of you. I would conquer the weak creations who could not deserve your love and force them to self-destruct rather then burden you with their unworthiness. I would return to you in strength and give our whole only the strong," Luciel cried.

"My love is for all species and creation, Luciel. The whole has no concept of unworthy. That is developed in your conceit and keeps you apart from the whole. I welcome all parts of creation to the center, even the imbalances you have created," Marah answered.

"If your love is for all creations, why do you not share it with me? I have strived to make myself worthy of you," Luciel admitted.

"You are worthy, Luciel, and have always been in potential, but you took that reality away when you refused to share with all of us the progress of your assignment. Then you sought to glorify your own separate evolvement. Come back to your commune and give your thesis to us all, and you will be my love and my mate," Marah replied.

"Sacrifice the power and energy I control to the commune? How can I release what is held together only by my consciousness?"

"Sharing is not a sacrifice. It is the path to the sublime. It is the only path to me. Come to us with the report of all your conscious creations and we will assimilate them. Come with me that we may align each other and then all can celebrate our cosmic mating. You have always been a planned mate, but your impatience was your undoing. You could not wait for the aligned time of our union, and you wished to be the only mate I would have. Both are acts of separateness, not wholeness. Neither of us has the power alone that we could have together," Marah stated.

"But I have not achieved my maximum potential here yet. When I do, then I will come to you in gladness and glory," Luciel exclaimed.

"Come to me now, Luciel, or you will pass the moment aligned for us. Then you will learn the lesson of time wasted and the waste of your potential. Don't you wish to mate with me?" asked Marah.

"Yes, that is my greatest desire and my motivation for great powers, that I would be the only one suited for cosmic mating with you. Then I would create the time and prolong it," Luciel replied.

"You have developed potent powers and you are a worthy mate for me, but the first sacrifice of your Ego will be to return to me now on the direction of the commune and on my request. I have always loved you. I will lose part of my maximum potential if you do not cosmic mate with me now. I would not see you burn up in your own imbalance of the energy you have created. The crossroad is here, now. I cannot ask the commune to grant you any more delays," Marah uttered with passion.

"I want you so much that I burn with the ecstasy I imagine. However, I have not completed my collection or finished the testings. I wanted you to be proud of my thesis," Luciel admitted.

"Your testing of Earth is completed and your collection is outstanding. The seeds of all of it will come with your consciousness to be replanted in the whole. Your growth cycle has reached its potential growth and you need new alignment and great stimulation to achieve the new realms you love to explore. I am the center of your new path. Do I not stimulate you Luciel?" Marah covered him in the golden rays and the moonbeams overflowing from the chalice.

"Go, Father. Mate as I have and share love, for its Light is a greater energy source than either of us conceived. A power more potent than perfection," Lucien interjected.

"Let us go, Marah. I will return with you to the commune and leave Earth to the children. For the first time, Michael, I'm delighted to leave them in your care. That's the part of the family responsibility I leave with you as I leave with their Mother. Now you can envy me. Goodbye," said Luciel as he started shedding form to convert to energy.

"In giving Earth back to the children, you insure they will return her balanced to all of us. That is the destiny of this cycle of evolution. Goodbye my loves. Love only grows when it's shared. Earth is in need of the powerful Light you will shine on her. Your love is the Light that reflects the spiritual energy connection to the physical forms. It reflects the forms recircuiting the energy of matter's own path back to its spiritual essence. Farewell!" cried Marah.

Marah and Luciel departed, and Mariella and Lucien looked at Michael. "Luciel made the right choice, children. Mating with your Mother is one of my most treasured delights. We return to Earth to balance and to experience the Great Change: the whirlwind and fireworks of creation. Then we will recenter the new root race in rebirth. What an exciting path we will tread. Come, the seeds of all our futures are to be sown on Earth," Michael said in eager anticipation.

"Are you jealous of Luciel, Father? Mating with Mother while you mind the children?" Mariella sassed.

"There is no envy or jealousy on the planes of my consciousness. I look forward to all my assignments of evolution, and I am, just as my Father, proud to be part of my children's future. Besides, all of us close to the center share all the pleasures of cosmic matings. In my consciousness is the channel to receive all the pleasures and energy connections that Marah and Luciel's mating creates. We're very sharing in our commune," Michael said smiling.

"Now that Luciel will not interfere, we can all relax," Mariella admitted.

"Relax, enjoy Earth and place all parts of her in your consciousness, for there will lie the record of her past achievements and the seeds of the new ones. Relax now, for soon Earth will awe you with earthquakes and floods and great storms leading to her fluxes of rebirth. Flow with them. They will come in increasing frequency until the main pressure blows, and then you too will be tested. For in survival you must return to primitive animal instincts; then, by rerouting these instincts to the overself of higher energy, you demonstrate the reuniting of the spiritual to the physical. There are others of the root race returning to Earth and I return there too. We will support the rebirth together in the name of evolution. The Son of the Ancient One returns also to inspire the direct link between the physical worlds and the spiritual ones; of the man to the god who created him. Return to seek your future together. I will stay awhile to admire Luciel's collection of Earth art. I have always imagined its beauty, but even archangels can be awed by the glories of form. I will join you later on Earth," said Michael as he bade them farewell. Lucien and Mariella returned to the ship.

"You must have brought Mother to my Father. Very clever Mariella. Now you have freed me and freed our future. Patterns are changing, and I promise our patterns after Earth life will change. You are my cosmic mate and I will not part from you again. We will remain together after form incarnation, and I will return with you to the commune of our Mother," Lucien promised.

"I'll remember the future promises, but it's now in Earth time that we must consider. We're free of Luciel for now, but we must take the future in simple steps along our combined paths. We're not free of the Great Changes on Earth. Don't the polar changes frighten you?"

"Why, a simple polarity change is not frightening, but definitely defining. I am full of faith in our destiny, and you're full of doubts the moment your Father is gone. You do the recording and reflecting for both of us; let me arrange the surviving. Our planet Earth will be reborn as will we, and our children to follow. We will return to Earth soon, but come here first; I think you need recentering. I want you to meet our future with desire as well as understanding. Maybe some cosmic sex can focus you and facilitate that." Lucien grabbed Mariella.

> "How you do preach, Lucien.
> Straight is the path,
> and narrow is the way,
> as I lay with my brother,
> and fuck every day!" Mariella teased.

"Every day and every way. Say every way, Mariella." Lucien nibbled her neck.

"Every way Lucien, but don't bite my neck. Every way but that."

The End